1980—1989

Yearbooks in Science

1980–1989

ROBERT E. DUNBAR

Twenty-First Century Books
A Division of Henry Holt and Company
New York

Twenty-First Century Books
A Division of Henry Holt and Company, Inc.
115 West 18th Street
New York, NY 10011

Henry Holt® and colophon are trademarks of
Henry Holt and Company, Inc.
Publishers since 1866

Published in Canada by Fitzhenry & Whiteside Ltd.
195 Allstate Parkway, Markham, Ontario L3R 4T8

Library of Congress Cataloging-in-Publication Data
Yearbooks in science.
p.   cm.
Includes indexes.
Contents: 1900–1919 / Tom McGowen — 1920–1929 / David E. Newton — 1930–1939 / Nathan Aaseng — 1940–1949 / Nathan Aaseng — 1950–1959 / Mona Kerby — 1960–1969 / Tom McGowen — 1970–1979 / Geraldine Marshall Gutfreund — 1980–1989 / Robert E. Dunbar — 1990 and beyond / Herma Silverstein.
ISBN 0–8050–3431–5 (v. 1)
1. Science—History—20th century—Juvenile literature. 2. Technology—History—20th century—Juvenile literature. 3. Inventions—History—20th century—Juvenile literature. 4. Scientists—20th century—Juvenile literature. 5. Engineers—20th century—Juvenile literature. [1. Science—History—20th century. 2. Technology—History—20th century.]
Q126.4.Y43 1995
609'.04—dc20   95–17485
                                                                        CIP
                                                                        AC

ISBN 0–8050–3438–2
First Edition 1995
Printed in Mexico
All first editions are printed on acid-free paper ∞.
10 9 8 7 6 5 4 3 2 1

Cover design by James Sinclair
Interior design by Kelly Soong

Cover photo credits
Background: Eruption of Mount Saint Helens, © Kraft-Explorer/Science Source/Photo Researchers, Inc.
Inset images (clockwise from right): Solar corona, © Michael O'Brine/Tom Stack & Associates; Lyme disease germ, © CDC/Science Source/Photo Researchers, Inc.; Toxic warning sign created by James Sinclair; El Niño, NASA GSFC/Science Photo Library/Photo Researchers, Inc.; the spread of radiation from Chernobyl, © Department of Energy/Photo Researchers, Inc.; cleanup following the *Exxon Valdez* spill, © Vanessa Vick/Photo Researchers, Inc.

Photo credits
p. 10: © Pat & Tom Leeson/Photo Researchers, Inc.; p. 13: © Susan Greenwood/Gamma-Liaison; p. 16: © 1978 F. Gohier/Photo Researchers, Inc.; p. 18: photo by Miriam Westervelt/Courtesy of Roger Tory Peterson Institute, Jamestown, NY; p. 20: Harvard University/Office of News and Public Affairs; p. 22, 53, 64: UPI/Bettmann; p. 24: Dudley Foster/Woods Hole Oceanographic Institution; p. 25: © Mark Newman/Tom Stack & Associates; p. 27: Reuters/Bettmann Newsphotos; page 31 (left): American Society for Microbiology; page 31 (right): Courtesy of Genentech, Inc.; p. 34: © Rich Miller/Gamma-Liaison; p. 35: UPI/Bettmann Newsphotos; p. 38: John Bavosi/Science Photo Library/Photo Researchers, Inc.; p. 39: © OMIKRON/Photo Researchers, Inc.; p. 44:Courtesy of Lincoln Mercury Division/Ford Motor Company; p. 45: Courtesy of International Business Machines Corporation; p. 50: North Wind Picture Archives; p. 55: © Eurotunnel/Q A Photos Ltd.; p. 58: NASA/Mark Marten/Photo Researchers, Inc.; p. 61: D. Connolly/Gamma-Liaison; p. 67: Photo European Space Agency; p. 68: Royal Observatory, Edinburgh/SPL/Photo Researchers, Inc.; p. 71: © W. Kaufmann/Jet Propulsion Laboratory/Science Source/Photo Researchers, Inc.

May science lead the way to world peace

Contents

1 THE NATURAL WORLD   9

2 MEDICINE   29

3 COMPUTERS   43

4 TECHNOLOGY   49

5 SPACE   57

     FURTHER READING   73

     INDEX   75

1

THE NATURAL WORLD

Much of the scientific activity of the 1980s was directed at studying changes in the environment, both changes that occur naturally and those inflicted by humans that posed threats to the health of people of all ages. Of particular concern were reports and predictions about the "greenhouse effect," a result of the thinning of the ozone layer in the atmosphere. Scientists theorized that this would allow more ultraviolet radiation to strike the earth, threatening the health of humans and all other forms of life. It would also produce a warming effect that would be harmful if temperatures continued to rise, with drastic changes in world climates and other alarming consequences.

Still more dangers to the environment were posed by the careless disposal of toxic wastes and the pollution of air and water. One of the worst air pollution tragedies occurred in India when a deadly gas used in the manufacture of pesticides was accidentally released into the air and killed 3,500 people. A similar tragedy, this one caused by nature and not by human carelessness, occurred in Africa. An underwater landslide in a beautiful lake in Cameroon released clouds of noxious gases into the surrounding area, killing hundreds of people.

MOUNT SAINT HELENS ERUPTS

When Mount Saint Helens erupted on May 18, 1980, there had been early warnings by the United States Geological Survey that this might happen. Because of those warnings, the number of lives lost was probably much lower than it might otherwise have been. Mount Saint Helens is one of fifteen active volcanoes in the Cascade Mountain Range in Washington State. It has erupted six times since the year 1700, almost 300 years ago. Of these fifteen active volcanoes, only six others have erupted since 1800.

A huge cloud of ash hangs over Mount Saint Helens after the eruption on May 18, 1980.

Because of recent advances in science, it was possible to make an ongoing detailed analysis of the effects the May 1980 eruption had on the environment, not only in the immediate vicinity of Mount Saint Helens but throughout the United States and other parts of the world as well. The results of these studies may make it possible to predict more accurately when a volcano will erupt in the future and what the consequences might be.

For instance, one of the techniques used to monitor and predict the activity of a volcano is to measure the emission rates and composition of the gas that emerges from a volcano when it erupts. Immediately after Mount Saint Helens erupted, gas emissions varied from hundreds to thousands of tons per day. Among the gases given off by the volcano were carbon dioxide and sulfur dioxide. Mount Saint Helens erupted several more times during 1980 and 1981, spewing more gas and ash into the air.

EFFECTS ON WEATHER

Climatologists, scientists who study the causes and results of weather, were deeply concerned about the eruptions of Mount Saint Helens. They were anxious about the effects these eruptions might have on climate and weather. Almost two centuries ago, in 1816, many parts of the world experienced the "year without a summer." This phenomenon was believed to be caused by contaminants thrown into the atmosphere by erupting volcanoes. The volcanoes produced a dense blanket of gases and debris that blocked out and diluted the sun's rays, energy, and warmth. The primary cause of the phenomenon was believed to be a series of volcanic explosions in the East Indies and Southeast Asia from 1813 to 1816. However, the eruptions of Mount Saint Helens caused only a temporary local increase in clouds and rainfall.

It took more than a decade for the Mount Saint Helens area to return to a semblance of its former self, but return it did. By May 1993, thirteen years after the eruption, the United States Forest Service opened the Coldwater Ridge Visitor Center at Mount Saint Helens. As one visitor, Susan Hauser, recounted in an article in the *New York Times*, "My visit became a celebration, a joyful greeting to the now plentiful signs of life that were absent for so long." She lived in Portland, Oregon, 50 miles (80 kilometers) to the south, and had witnessed the eruption in 1980.

Below the Visitor Center is Coldwater Lake, formerly a tiny creek, which the eruption transformed into an 800-acre (320-hectare) lake. The lake now abounds in trout that were stocked in 1989. No birds or large mammals in the Mount Saint Helens area survived the blast. However, some amphibians (animals that can live in water or on land) survived and so did insects and small mammals that were underground. Eventually they emerged through the thick residue of volcanic ash.

In the years that followed, more animals returned to the area. They brought spores and seeds that produced new plant life. One of the remark-

---

THE YEAR WITHOUT A SUMMER

The year was 1816 and it was long remembered as the "year without a summer" or the "black year." In Europe, it was known as the "famine year" because of the widespread effect on crops and livestock that led to food shortages. An account published by the Maine Geological Society stated: "January, 1816, was unusually mild but May arrived with wintry temperatures. Buds froze and ice formed on ponds and streams. Ohio had snow that month and frost occurred as far south as Virginia.

"June brought sleet and snow. It was reported that on July 4th 'ice as thick as window glass formed throughout New England, New York and in some parts of Pennsylvania.' Scientists believe that a combination of sun spots and volcanic dust from the 1815 eruption of Mt. Tamboro, a volcano located on the island of Sumbawa in Indonesia, caused the phenomenal weather that unsummery summer."

able results of this rebirth of life was the return of herds of elk that are now among the largest in Washington State.

THE IMPORTANCE OF EL NIÑO

The elusive nature of weather plagues scientists who try to understand and predict weather events of major consequence. As the decade of the 1980s moved into its middle years, a phenomenon called El Niño drew major attention because of its worldwide effects on weather. El Niño is a massive warming of the surface waters of the tropical eastern Pacific Ocean. This results in a spectacular interaction between the ocean and the atmosphere.

El Niño began in late 1982 and continued into much of 1983. This extreme weather event occurs from time to time but as yet has been unpredictable. The 1982–1983 event, however, was the strongest scientists had ever recorded. Many believed it might be the most extensive climatic phenomenon of the century.

One of the unusual characteristics of El Niño in 1983 was its buildup over a long period of time. Consequently it released huge amounts of heat and energy into the atmosphere. This created major changes in global weather circulation. Wind patterns, pressure, and large-scale rainfall shifted eastward. Areas that were normally dry experienced heavy rainfall. The reverse was true in wet areas. Many parts of Australia and Indonesia were deprived of their normal rainfall. Other areas experienced abnormally dry weather as well, among them the Philippines, South Africa, southern India, and Sri Lanka.

Several other disturbing weather events may have been influenced by El Niño, such as record high temperatures in Siberia, cold and snow in the Middle East, wet weather in southern China, and flooding in western Europe. In the United States in 1983, there was warm winter weather east of the Rocky Mountains, huge snowfalls in the Northeast in January and February, and a heat wave and drought over much of the United States from July to September.

HURRICANE HUGO HITS

On an intensity scale of one to five, one being the lowest and five the highest, Hurricane Hugo registered four and became the most destructive and costly

A satellite image gives clear indications of the intensity of Hurricane Hugo.

storm to strike the United States up to that time. Hugo's destruction began September 17, 1989, when it hit the island of Guadeloupe in the eastern Caribbean. The storm moved on to Saint Croix and Puerto Rico, then to the eastern seaboard of the United States. By September 21, when it reached Charleston, South Carolina, Hugo's wind power continued to maintain a high of 140 miles (225 kilometers) per hour. Storm tides reached a height of 20 feet (6 meters).

Hurricane Hugo claimed seventy-one lives and caused an estimated $8.6 million in damage. However, scientific predictions and warnings by alert meteorologists saved an untold number of lives. One estimate stated that more than half a million people from Savannah, Georgia, to Cape Hatteras, North Carolina, heeded the hurricane warnings and evacuated their coastal and barrier island homes.

THE GREENHOUSE EFFECT

The reported increase in carbon dioxide in the atmosphere caused by the burning of coal in manufacturing plants and the combustion of gasoline by automobiles, trucks, and other sources worried scientists in the decade of the 1980s. They feared a potential greenhouse effect, or unnatural warming of the earth.

In the United States, the Environmental Protection Agency (EPA) warned that the average world temperature might rise 3.6°F (2°C) by the year 2040, and 9°F (5°C) by the end of the twenty-first century.

The EPA recommended the prohibition of carbon dioxide emissions and the injection of sulfur dioxide into the stratosphere to induce climatic cooling. The stratosphere is the second layer of the atmosphere, about 7 miles (11 kilometers) or more above the earth. There are four other layers. These include the troposphere, which is in contact with the earth's surface, and three layers above the stratosphere: the mesosphere, the thermosphere, and the exosphere. The EPA also recommended a large-scale increase in forests. Trees take in carbon dioxide and give off oxygen. Forests would help increase the amount of oxygen in the atmosphere.

Evidence in support of the existence of the greenhouse effect was offered in March 1984 by two British scientists, Philip Jones and Mick Kelly of the Climatic Research Unit in the United Kingdom. Jones and Kelly presented evidence that showed that the Northern Hemisphere was indeed warming and that this greenhouse effect was caused by the release of too much carbon dioxide.

MORE EVIDENCE OF THE GREENHOUSE EFFECT

In 1987, Donald Graybill of the University of Arizona Tree Ring Laboratory in Tucson reported a continuing increase in the growth rate of bristlecone pines in a huge area encompassing 386,000 square miles (1,003,600 square kilometers) of the United States. According to Graybill, the increase was due to large amounts of carbon dioxide in the air.

The effect of increasing amounts of carbon dioxide in the atmosphere was also noted by botanist Frank Woodward of the University of Cambridge, England. When he examined plants that had been stored in an herbarium for more than 200 years, Woodward discovered that in several species the number of stomata, the tiny pores in leaves and stems, had been reduced due to increases in the carbon dioxide content of the air.

Still another claim of harmful results attributed to the greenhouse effect came from meteorologists in the United States and England. They reported increases in rain and snow in the midlatitudes (latitudes of the temperate zones) of the United States, Europe, and the Soviet Union over the past several decades. At the same time, rainfall in the subtropics had declined. In each instance, scientists claimed the conditions were consistent with predictions of what the greenhouse effect could produce.

HOLES IN THE OZONE LAYER

Ozone is a gas consisting of molecules that contain three oxygen atoms. A layer of this gas can be found from 6 to 30 miles (10 to 48 kilometers) above the earth's surface. Without the shielding power of this ozone layer, humans and other forms of life would be exposed to harmful concentrations of ultraviolet radiation from the sun. This exposure can cause skin cancer, cataracts, and damage to the human immune system, as well as disruption of all parts of the earth and its atmosphere that are capable of supporting life.

Scientists had worried for a long time about the thinning of the ozone layer caused by chemical compounds known as chlorofluorocarbons, or CFCs. These compounds were once widely used as spray can propellants, refrigeration coolants, and in many industrial products and processes. They have also been blamed for contributing to the greenhouse effect.

Cries of alarm reached a high pitch in 1985 when a "hole" in the ozone layer was discovered over Antarctica and, three years later, over the Arctic. By the end of 1988, thirty-one nations had ratified the Montreal Protocol, adopted by the United Nations. This agreement called for a gradual reduction in the use of chlorinated compounds through the 1990s, leading eventually to complete stoppage.

CONCERN ABOUT THE RAIN FORESTS OF THE AMAZON

The huge area in South America known as the rain forest of the Amazon is a thick jungle of trees, bushes, and other vegetation. It teems with thousands of species of plant and animal life, many of them rare and still unknown to scientists. Those who are deeply concerned with protecting the environment of the world as a whole see the Amazon rain forests as a huge verdant lung whose trees supply oxygen that all life, including human life, must have to survive.

Many tropical areas of the world contain rain forests, but the Amazon rain forest is the largest, encompassing about one-fourth of Brazil's land-

*A caiman, photographed on
the banks of a Brazilian river*

mass. It also reaches into parts of eight surrounding countries: Bolivia, Peru, Ecuador, Colombia, Venezuela, Guyana, Suriname, and French Guiana. Situated on mostly flatland, the rain forest of the Amazon stretches from the Atlantic Ocean in the east to the Andes Mountains in the west.

Alarmingly, by 1981, about one-third of the original Amazon rain forest had been sold off to developers who had felled trees and cleared the land for cultivation. Development of the land continued throughout the decade, with an area larger than Denmark and Switzerland combined—38,600 square miles (100,360 square kilometers)—cleared each year.

In most ecosystems, half or more of the minerals and other valuable nutrients are contained in the soil. But in a tropical rain forest, about 90 percent of the nutrients are blown away in smoke and ash produced by spontaneous forest fires caused by lightning, or wash away in rains. So the land that remains is not rich in nutrients to begin with. Once cultivated for crops or livestock grazing, the soil is quickly exhausted unless it receives huge amounts of fertilizer. Without fertilizer, the soil becomes a wasteland.

WHEN THE RAIN FOREST IS UNDISTURBED

In its natural state, the Amazon rain forest is one of nature's wonders. A little crocodile called a caiman feeds on fish that swim in the smaller rivers. The waste or excreta produced by caimans enriches the lakes that are fed by rising streams. These are the lakes where the fish that are the caimans' prey go to spawn.

Turtles feed on aquatic vegetation and pass on their nutrients to carnivorous fish that thrive on a diet that includes young turtles. Other fish feed directly on the forest itself. This happens from June to November, when the rivers of the Amazon create a floodplain of about 62,000 square miles (161,200 square kilometers). Fish migrate with the spreading water as it rises into the trees. They feed on falling seeds, nuts, and fruits. Many species of fish, including the flesh-eating piranha, have developed specially adapted molars that make it possible for them to crush nuts.

According to plant geneticists, scientists who study the genetic makeup or characteristics of plants, certain plants and trees now commonly cultivated in other areas of the world have their origins in rain forests. These include trees and plants that produce coffee, rubber, tea, and cocoa. Cultivated strains of these and hundreds of other plant species need new genetic material from the wild to maintain healthy growth. West African cocoa breeders were highly pleased with the results when they crossed domestic plants with wild and semiwild strains of the cacao plant from the Upper Amazon. The new plants were much healthier and more productive.

The hardiness of trees that flourish for decades in the Amazon rain forest also intrigued plant geneticists in 1981. One of the reasons for the trees' long life is their bark, which contains chemicals that are powerful insecticides and fungicides. In an address to the British Ecological Society, Clifford Evans, a botanist, declared that studies of relations of insects to the barks of rain forest trees would provide the basis for a whole new generation of agricultural insecticides.

The growth of fungus on trees and other plants can destroy them and so can the invasion of insects. By using chemicals like those found in the bark of Amazon rain forest trees, new insecticides and fungicides could be produced to protect other trees and plants.

100,000 BIRDSONG RECORDINGS

Scientists had been recording birdsongs for almost a century by 1981. In all, 100,000 recordings had been made of 5,000 bird species, more than half of the 9,000 species known to exist. These recordings are used to identify birds both in the field and in the laboratory. They are also used in studies of bird behavior and development, learning ability, heredity, and in pest control.

Scientists who study birdsongs are called ornithological sound specialists. Their goal at the start of the decade was to record as many tropical bird species as possible, especially those in lowland rain forests that would probably be extinct by the end of the century. One new species discovered in Peru in 1981 was the cloud forest screech owl (*Otus marshalli*). Another major event that year was a new edition of Roger Tory Peterson's *Field Guide to the Birds*, the best-selling bird book ever published.

ROGER TORY PETERSON

When Roger Tory Peterson was eleven years old and living in Jamestown, New York, he began an interest in birds that has lasted all his life and brought him worldwide fame as an author and artist. The first edition of his famous book, *Field Guide to the Birds*, covering eastern and central North America, was published in 1934, when he was twenty-six years old. Many editions later, this book has sold millions of copies.

However, Peterson didn't start out to be a writer. He had a natural talent as an artist, a talent he later combined with his writing about birds. When he was seventeen years old, he enrolled at the Art Students League in New York City, studying under a famous painter, John Sloan.

Roger Tory Peterson

Through his interest in birds, he developed and perfected his interest in nature painting. By the time he was seventy, still active as a writer and painter, Roger Tory Peterson had painted more than 4,000 birds. Many of his bird paintings and drawings were published in his *Field Guide* and in other books.

THE ENDANGERED ELEPHANT?

Alarmed at claims that many elephant herds were facing extinction, the watchdog group known as CITES (Convention on International Trade in Endangered Species of Wild Fauna and Flora) in October 1989 classified the elephant as an endangered species. In Africa alone, there had been a massive decline in the elephant population, reported to number only 625,000 animals. The persistent demand for the ivory that comes from elephant tusks had officials worried about the threat the sale of ivory posed to the elephants' ability to reproduce themselves in large numbers. Even so, five countries, including two African nations, Zimbabwe and Botswana, said they would continue to trade in ivory.

Claims by CITES and other wildlife conservation organizations that the elephant was endangered were strongly denied in an article by Raymond Bonner published in the *New York Times*, February 7, 1993, titled "Crying Wolf Over Elephants." Although there were only 800 elephants in Kenya's Amboseli National Park in 1993, that was more than the park could handle, according to famed elephant researcher Cynthia Moss.

Exclaimed Bonner: "The park has been ravaged by the elephants; it looks like someone has dropped napalm [a firebomb] on it, the trees dead and dying. Because of the loss of their habitat, there are fewer impala, giraffes, bushbabies, and monkeys; kudus, bushbucks, and genet have disappeared. Everyone agrees, including Moss and Leakey (Richard Leakey, head of the Kenya Wildlife Service) that the number of elephants must be reduced or at least controlled."

Bonner also pointed out in his article that elephants in Botswana, Zimbabwe, and South Africa, far from being endangered, were increasing in numbers. In Botswana, the number had doubled in ten years to 56,000. In Zimbabwe, they had increased from 30,000 in 1979 to 52,000 in 1993. "It is true that Kenya's elephant population has declined sharply, to about 20,000," he wrote. "But given the country's growing human population and its need for land on which to grow food, that is the maximum number of elephants the country can tolerate."

CHARLES DARWIN AND EVOLUTION

Charles Darwin, the scientist who amazed the world with his theory of evolution, died in 1882. In honor of the one hundredth anniversary of Darwin's death, a series of conferences about his theories were held in many parts of the world in 1982. A number of the conferences focused on Darwin's theory of natural selection. According to Darwin, natural selection is nature's way of determining how plant and animal species change over long periods of time. In most cases, the plants and animals that survive are those that are best fitted to survive under the conditions in which they live. Darwin called this concept the principle of survival of the fittest.

A century after his death, most evolutionary biologists still consider some of Darwin's theories and ideas sound. However, there are scientists who strongly disagree with his basic ideas. One of them is biologist Stephen Jay Gould. For example, Gould has expressed disagreement with the concept that natural selection alone determines the results of evolution. Instead he puts special emphasis on hereditary or genetic factors in determining whether plants, animals, or any other forms of life will survive.

GETTING RID OF POISONS SAFELY

The problem of getting rid of poisonous industrial wastes and other toxins was one of the major concerns of environmental scientists during the 1980s. In 1983, an international firm, Hoffman-LaRoche, which operates in the United States as well as in Europe, drew severe criticism. Forty-one barrels of dioxin-contaminated waste from one of LaRoche's subsidiary plants in Italy had been discovered in a slaughterhouse in northern France. Officials there said they had signed an agreement with a German company to get rid of the waste safely, but this had not been done. Finally, a Swiss firm, Ciba-Geigy AG, agreed to do what the German firm had failed to do, dispose of the hazardous waste.

Dioxin is the name of a family, or group, of poisonous substances. It is one of the deadliest toxic wastes known to man. It is at least 10,000 times more dangerous than cyanide. It causes acute skin disease and is suspected of causing cancer. Dioxin was one of the ingredients in Agent Orange, the chemical used to defoliate areas in South Vietnam during the Vietnam War. Many soldiers who were exposed to Agent Orange have alleged they suffered ill health effects because of it, including liver disease and cancer. Many of these veterans have had children with birth defects.

The problem with this toxic waste continued well into the 1990s. In a letter to the *New York Times*, published on September 29, 1994, Floyd Hasselriis, a consulting engineer in combustion and pollution control, pointed to the dioxin hazards in recycling of waste, in particular scrap metal. He wrote: "Metal smelting and refining, particularly the recycling of iron, steel, aluminum, and lead scrap, are prime suspects for dioxin. While 'trash-to-energy' plants can almost eliminate dioxin emissions, it is well within the realm of possibility that metal recycling is the number 1 dioxin source in the United States."

The best disposal method for this particular toxic waste is to burn it at extremely high temperatures. A specialized incinerator is needed, with the capacity to maintain temperatures as high as 2,372°F (1,300°C).

In 1983, there were five other methods of toxic waste disposal: disposal at sea; landfills (burial underground); long-term storage; chemical; and biological treatment, with the treated residues buried in landfills. For example, in 1983, a biotechnologist, Ananda Chakrabarty, was working with a particular type of organism at Love Canal in Niagara Falls, New York—organisms that have the ability to degrade or break down dioxin and other toxic chemicals. Love Canal was declared a major disaster area because of heavy contamination by dioxin and other poisonous substances in residential areas during the 1970s and 1980s. It was Chakrabarty who had patented the first genetically engineered microorganism that was specifically designed to degrade oil spills.

THE HAZARDS OF ACID RAIN

Environmental problems continued uppermost in the minds of many scientists in 1984. Of major concern were the harmful effects of acid rain. One report stated that more than one-third of the forests in West Germany had been damaged by acid rain. The acidic rain was believed to be caused in part by sulfur dioxide and nitrogen emissions as well as by fuel-generated pollutants. There were reports of acid rain damage in forests and lakes in many other parts of the world, including the United States.

In August 1984, New York became the first state to enact legislation against acid rain. Scientists were commissioned to identify those areas of the state that were most at risk. The scientists were also responsible for determining what levels of air pollution these areas would be able to tolerate without serious damage. The new law stated that by 1988, rules were to be put into effect to minimize the harmful effects of the industrial burning of oil and coal, one of the main contributors to the creation of acid rain.

TOXIC GAS TRAGEDY IN INDIA

Late in 1984, on December 3, the world's worst industrial disaster struck in Bhopal, India, when 50 tons (45 metric tons) of methyl isocyanate gas, produced as a pesticide, were accidentally released from a plant owned by an

Residents gather outside the Union Carbide factory in Bhopal, India, following the disaster there in December 1984.

Indian subsidiary of the Union Carbide Corporation, a United States firm. The escaping gas quickly spread throughout the surrounding residential area, killing many people instantly. Panic ensued as thousands of people attempted to flee. By December 15, the death toll had reached 1,300. An estimated 100,000 others had been injured and were receiving treatment.

When the heads of Union Carbide and its Indian subsidiary arrived in Bhopal to investigate, they were arrested by local authorities. Later, however, Warren Anderson, Union Carbide's chief executive officer, was allowed to return to the United States. Lawsuits amounting to billions of dollars were filed in the United States on behalf of the tragedy's victims.

The final death toll in Bhopal, India, was 3,500 people. The Indian government dropped criminal charges against Union Carbide; however, the company agreed to pay $470 million in settlement of claims filed against it.

A "GOOD LAKE" TURNS BAD

For many years, the people of Cameroon in Africa called Lake Nyos in the northwest the "good lake." Its clear blue waters filled the crater of a long-dormant volcano. But in 1986, Lake Nyos became the site of the worst geophysical disaster of the year. On the evening of August 21, a huge rumbling cloud of noxious gases arose from the lake. Most of the gas cloud consisted of carbon dioxide, but it also contained smaller amounts of two poisonous gases, carbon monoxide and hydrogen sulfide. However, it was the carbon dioxide that proved deadliest.

Carbon dioxide is a part of air, and slightly heavier than oxygen. When carbon dioxide accumulates in an unusually large amount, as it did at Lake Nyos, it displaces oxygen and can cause death by asphyxiation. The people who lived in the area surrounding Lake Nyos were caught unaware by the mass of gases as it rolled down the slopes of the volcano. Because the incident happened at night, many people were asleep in their beds. Even those who were awake, however, were unable to escape in time. The death toll reached 1,706, and thousands of others within a 10-mile (16-kilometer) area were injured. Almost all of the livestock in that area were killed.

Scientists who investigated the tragedy believed that the gases seeped slowly from cracks or vents in the floor of the crater beneath the lake. The gases remained trapped there until released by turbulence and vertical currents that were caused by an underwater landslide. This brought them quickly to the surface and into the air, and tragedy followed.

LIFE AT THE OCEAN BOTTOM

Most forms of life on earth need sunlight, either direct or indirect, to thrive and survive. Plants use pigments such as the green in chlorophyll to trap and transform radiant energy from the sun. This process produces life-sustaining carbohydrates from carbon dioxide and water. Plants could not survive without sunlight, nor could the animals that feed on plants. Human beings and some other forms of life feed on both plants and animals. This same dependence of plant and animal life on sunlight for survival also exists in the ocean, with certain remarkable exceptions.

One of these is the riftia, a meter-long worm that lives within a tube-shaped body from which it waves a blood-red plume. These worms were first discovered in 1977 by a small research submarine called *Alvin*. At the time, *Alvin* was exploring the sea floor where new crust was being formed as the result of volcanic eruptions.

The hot lava from the eruptions not only warmed the seawater to a temperature of 50°F (10°C), it also released minerals, including sulfides and dissolved oxygen. This was the source of the riftia's life-sustaining nutrients. When sulfide combines with oxygen, it becomes sulfate, creating energy that can be used by the riftia worms to survive and grow.

Riftia worms were just one of the startling new life-forms discovered by the research submarine Alvin.

By 1988, full knowledge of the origin of the riftia and how they were able to colonize the energy-rich sea vent area was still eluding scientists. However, one fact was clear enough: the existence of riftia and other forms of life nourished by sea vents showed just how tenacious life-forms can be whenever they have access to an energy source and water.

OIL SPILLS—A MAJOR THREAT TO THE ENVIRONMENT

When the oil tanker *Exxon Valdez* ran aground in Prince William Sound, Alaska, on March 24, 1989, about 200,000 barrels of crude oil were spilled into the ocean. Cleanup crews were rushed to the scene but were able to recover only 3,000 barrels of the spilled oil. The inadequacy of the cleanup response and the overwhelming threat to fish and other marine life, as well as to seabirds and the immediate environment, underscored the need for new, more efficient technology for dealing with oil spills.

Technology then in effect included the use of booms, skimmers, dispersants, and other chemical treatments. Booms are mechanical barriers that are designed to keep oil at the site of a spill and prevent it from spreading. This can sometimes keep an oil spill from reaching areas where it could harm natural resources, such as marshes and oyster beds. Usually a boom consists of a flotation device, a structure called a tension member designed to maintain the boom's shape against currents, waves, and high winds, plus a skirt that extends down into the water to help keep the oil in place. Once the spilled oil has been isolated in this way, skimmers can be used to recover the oil from the surface of the water.

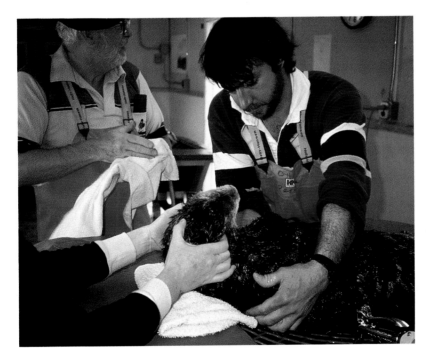

Despite the best efforts of volunteers and others, the loss of wildlife following the Exxon Valdez *oil spill was considerable. Workers shown here are cleaning oil from an otter.*

Dispersants and other chemical treatments are used to break up an oil slick into small droplets. This helps prevent the oil from contaminating birds, fish eggs, and other surface organisms. It also helps to decompose the oil.

All of these methods were used to help prevent some of the harmful effects of oil spills in the 1980s, but none of them was completely successful. The best way to deal with oil spills, experts cautioned, was to prevent them from happening at all.

NUCLEAR DISASTER AT CHERNOBYL

The fear of a nuclear disaster with its threat to all forms of life is constant wherever a nuclear plant is built and operated. That fear became a reality at 1:23 A.M., April 26, 1986, when a runaway nuclear reaction occurred at the Chernobyl nuclear plant in Chernobyl, Belorussia, in the Soviet Union. It took only three seconds for the power output of the nuclear reactor to rise from 7 percent to 50 percent of full power. When this happened, the fuel elements burst apart.

This placed the superheated fuel particles in direct contact with the cooling water, which was immediately transformed into steam. In turn, this caused a pressure shock that blew off the top of the reactor vessel and the roof of the building. At the same time, the servicing crane came crashing down on the reactor.

When the fuel elements and cooling tubes ruptured, the resulting steam came in direct contact with the zirconium coating on the fuel elements and the graphite blocks that surrounded the cooling tubes. This reaction produced hydrogen. As soon as the hydrogen was exposed to the atmosphere, it ignited, causing fires that burned out of control for nearly four hours.

Fires were only one result of the disaster at Chernobyl. The radioactive particles injected into the atmosphere were spread over much of Scandinavia as well as eastern and central Europe. Livestock, milk, meat, and other foodstuffs from these areas had to be destroyed because of the feared contamination. The potential threat to humans was also alarming. Initial reports attributed two deaths to the explosion. Because of high radiation levels, 135,000 people living within 300 square miles (780 square kilometers) of the plant were evacuated.

According to investigators, the Chernobyl nuclear power plant accident could be traced to two causes. One was the poor design of the nuclear reactor itself, which had control problems. The other was the plant operators' deliberate disregard of established safety procedures.

The plant operators had been running a test to see how long the steam turbines would operate while coasting to a stop when the reactor was shut off. This would tell them how much time they would have to put emergency safety systems into effect.

However, because of the length of time that the reactor was operating at low levels, it took almost two hours to get the power output to the desired level. By then, almost all of the safety features of the reactor had been disconnected or turned off.

When the operators blocked off further emergency protection signals in order to repeat the test, the flow of steam to the turbine was shut off, and the turbine began to slow to a stop. The circulation pumps also slowed, and so did the flow of coolant to the reactor.

The temperature rose sharply in the fuel channels of the reactor because of its design, putting the reactor out of control. It was not until the end of September, five months after the explosion, that any of the undamaged reactors were able to produce power again, and by then the total cost of the disaster was several billion dollars.

Three years later, Russian officials continued to be troubled about the results of the incident at Chernobyl. Plans were announced for evacuating

Lieutenant Colonel Leonid Telyatnikov, head of the fire brigade that fought the Chernobyl blaze, points at a photograph of the power station's damaged reactor. Telyatnikov, hospitalized with acute radiation sickness for two months after the nuclear accident, was twice decorated for bravery.

103,000 people from areas in two provinces where high levels of cesium-137, an element used in electron tubes, had been recorded. Reports also showed an increase in farm animals born deformed at a collective farm 31 miles (50 kilometers) southwest of Chernobyl. Also noted was an increase in chronic illnesses among humans and a doubling of new cancer cases, in particular cancers of the lip and thyroid gland.

By 1992, a study of the effects of radiation among children affected by the Chernobyl disaster pointed to the incidence of thyroid cancer. The study produced the first reliable data in the population downwind of the 1986 Chernobyl accident. According to Dr. Vasily S. Kazakov of the Belarus Ministry of Health in Minsk and his colleagues, thyroid cancer rates began to soar in 1990 in the regions most heavily affected by the radiation.

The city of Gomel, 140 miles (225 kilometers) north of Chernobyl, was used as an example. Before the nuclear accident, there used to be one or two cases of thyroid cancer a year, but in 1991 alone there were 38 cases. In the city of Minsk and six regions of Belarus, there were 131 cases of thyroid cancer in young children. Some of them were still in their mother's womb when the Chernobyl accident happened.

2

MEDICINE

Developments in genetic engineering continued to dominate medical news in the 1980s. So did news of a deadly virus called AIDS, which soon became an epidemic, seemingly out of control and threatening the lives of humans of all ages and sexual orientations.

First identified as a killer disease in 1981, by 1982 AIDS was claiming hundreds, and soon thousands, of victims. In addition, it was found in supplies of donated blood used in surgery and in the treatment of certain diseases. Those who were afflicted with the bleeding disease called hemophilia were particularly vulnerable to infected blood supplies.

Among other medical highlights of the decade were efforts to prevent heart attacks by giving heart disease patients medication that lowered their cholesterol levels. One study showed how aspirin could be used as a heart attack preventive, but it was not without serious drawbacks. A more practical method of preventing heart attacks was introduced by two West German scientists who had developed a technique to stop heart attacks before they could do major damage to affected heart muscle.

NOBEL PRIZES IN CHEMISTRY AND MEDICINE

In 1980, Nobel Prizes, the highest honors awarded for achievements in science, were presented to researchers in the United States, Great Britain, and France for their work in chemistry and physiology or medicine. Awards for chemistry went to Paul Berg and Walter Gilbert of the United States and Frederick Sanger of Great Britain, honored for their work in genetic engineering. They showed how bacteria can be programmed to synthesize or duplicate human proteins and other desirable molecules.

Because of their work, manufacturers were able to produce human interferon from bacteria. Interferon is a natural substance produced by the human body to destroy viruses when they invade cells. The work of Berg, Gilbert, and Sanger made it possible to produce interferon for use in the treatment of viral infections. Viral infections had been particularly difficult to treat because they do not respond to antibiotics.

The Nobel Prize for physiology or medicine went to George Snell and Baruj Benacerraf of the United States and Jean Dausset of France. All three men had been able to discover much of the genetic basis that causes the body's immune system to reject grafted or transplanted organs, such as the liver, kidney, and heart. More importantly, their work brought new explanations of why some people have an inherited resistance to such disabling illnesses as rheumatoid arthritis, multiple sclerosis, and diabetes, while others do not.

GENE SPLICING

A revolutionary new way of manipulating DNA, the genetic material of all living organisms, was discovered in 1973 by Stanley Cohen of Stanford University in Palo Alto, California, and Herbert Boyer of the University of California at San Francisco. Called gene splicing or recombinant DNA technology, this technique made it possible to remove segments of DNA from one organism and splice them into the genome, or gene set, of another. Gene splicing was intended as a tool for research, but it did not take scientists long to realize its potential for practical applications.

By 1980, the technique was in high gear commercially. Manufacturers were genetically programming bacteria to produce human proteins. Most of the efforts were concentrated on three essential products: insulin, interferon, and human growth hormone.

The gene-splicing method of making human insulin, essential in the treatment of diabetes, was developed by Genentech, Inc., of San Francisco for the Eli Lilly pharmaceutical company. Clinical trials were being made in London, England, in July 1980 as the first step in obtaining approval of the drug from the U.S. Food and Drug Administration.

Genentech had also developed a gene-splicing method for producing interferon, used in the treatment of viral infections. Other manufacturers

Stanley Cohen (left) *and Herbert Boyer developed the gene splicing technique that would revolutionize the field of genetics.*

were working to produce human growth hormone by the gene-splicing method for use in the treatment of dwarfism.

THE WORLD'S FIRST TEST TUBE TWINS

One of medicine's sensational happenings in 1980 was the announcement by scientists at the Queen Victoria Medical Centre in Melbourne, Australia, that they had been successful in producing the world's first test tube twins. The prospective mother was given hormones that caused her to release several eggs instead of the usual one egg that is released during a woman's monthly menstrual period. All of the eggs were then fertilized.

Two of the embryos that resulted were implanted in the mother's womb. This was done in order to increase the chances for success. If one was not successful, the other might be. But in this case, both were successful, producing the world's first test tube twins.

The embryos that were not used were frozen and stored in liquid nitrogen in the event the first attempt at implantation had failed. They remained in storage and, according to one of the scientists, could survive for 400 years. This raised a very uncomfortable question of medical ethics, namely, what should be done with the embryos?

Stopping a Heart Attack

Most heart attacks occur when a blood clot blocks an artery leading to the heart, thus cutting off its blood supply. The heart muscle, which depends on a continuous supply of blood to keep it healthy and strong, will die unless the blood supply is restored quickly. This makes it vitally important for doctors to do whatever they can to dissolve the blood clot in the shortest amount of time possible.

There is no way of predicting just how long a heart attack will last, but most heart attacks last from twelve to twenty-four hours. About half of the heart cells affected by the lack of an adequate blood supply will die in the first few hours.

Acting on this knowledge, two West German doctors, Peter Rentrop and Karl Karsh, found they could stop a heart attack when they threaded a catheter, a narrow plastic tube, into the blocked coronary artery and injected the enzyme streptokinase to dissolve the blood clot. They found that this stopped the patient's chest pains. When the patient was given an electrocardiogram to see how his or her heart was functioning, the heart rhythm had returned to normal. This indicated that the patient's heart was functioning properly.

By the 1990s, other drug therapies, including the use of injections into the veins to dissolve blood clots, had been developed. But streptokinase treatments continued to be an important option, and much less expensive than some other drug therapies.

A Mysterious Disease Called AIDS

The medical community and the general public were shocked in 1981 with reports of a mysterious disease that killed 40 percent of its victims. The disease was initially identified as HIV or human immuno-deficiency virus and later called AIDS, or acquired immune deficiency syndrome. The disease caused a failure of the body's immune system, which normally fights off cancer and infection. Victims of AIDS were subject to cancer and a host of infections that their bodies were powerless to fight.

The largest group of persons infected with the disease initially was homosexual men; however, further investigation revealed that it was also infecting the heterosexual population. Of the 500 AIDS victims who had been identified by late 1982, there were 27 women and more than 60 men who said they were not homosexual.

It seemed apparent to investigators that whatever the cause of the disease, it was being spread through sexual contact. Some researchers suggested it might be a virus that infiltrated the blood, semen, and other body fluids of its victims. This brought immediate attention, among other areas, to blood transfusions as a potential source of spreading the disease. There was an increased awareness of the need to promote safe sex—the use of condoms in sexual intercourse to protect each partner from infection. The speed with which the disease was spreading alarmed public health specialists.

THE AIDS PANIC

By 1983, the number of known AIDS cases in the United States had more than tripled, from 500 to 1,600, and the disease was spreading in Great Britain and other European countries as well as in Africa. Each day, four or five new cases were reported, and the death rate was very high. This created a panic. Patients who needed blood transfusions refused them for fear of contracting AIDS. The amount of blood available also decreased due to an unwillingness among many potential blood donors to give blood. They, too, feared AIDS infection, even though there was no evidence that by donating blood they would be at risk.

Undertakers who feared infection refused to accept the bodies of AIDS victims for embalming and burial. Many nurses and paramedics refused to touch patients who had AIDS. Fear of infection through contact with a patient's mouth made some dentists refuse treatment to people with AIDS. Because the largest single group of victims was homosexual men, many who were known to be homosexual were shunned by employers and landlords. The widespread prejudice against homosexuals and homosexual lifestyles brought accusations that the federal government was not doing enough to combat the epidemic and find a cure for the disease.

That charge was denied by officials who said the United States government was spending more on AIDS research in 1983 than had been spent in eight years of research on toxic shock syndrome and Legionnaires' disease combined. A total of $26.5 million had been allocated for AIDS research in 1983, with $14.5 million coming from the U.S. Department of Health and Human Services and $12 million in supplements voted by Congress. Twelve years later, in 1995, the AIDS research program at the National Institutes of Health had funding of $1.3 billion.

IDENTIFYING THE AIDS VIRUS

In 1984, researchers in the United States and France announced that they had identified a type of human cancer virus that apparently caused the acquired immune deficiency syndrome. This announcement came from Robert Gallo and his associates at the U.S. National Cancer Institute and from a team of French researchers at the Institute Pasteur in Paris. Gallo and his team identified the virus as human T cell lymphotropic virus, type III, or HTLV-III. The virus that the French identified, the same as or similar to HTLV-III, was designated LAV, or lymphadenopathy-associated virus.

In other major AIDS developments, the number of known cases had jumped to 6,600, and the projected life expectancy after diagnosis was two years. The search continued for an anti-AIDS vaccine, but the prospects were not encouraging. Equally urgent was the search for a method of determining if a blood sample contained the virus. This would make it possible for blood bank officials to screen donated blood so they could avoid unknowingly using AIDS-contaminated blood for transfusions.

THE FIGHT AGAINST AIDS CONTINUES

By 1985, it had been four years since AIDS had been identified, with the number of victims at least doubling in each of these four years. There were now almost 16,000 known cases of the acquired immune deficiency syndrome, and more than 8,000 Americans with AIDS had died. An estimated 50,000 to 100,000 others showed possible early signs of the disease, a condition known as the AIDS-related complex, or ARC. Another estimate was that as many as one million people in the United States had AIDS antibodies in their blood, indicating they had been exposed to the virus.

Ryan White and his mother are shown here in a photograph taken in 1987.

Of major concern was the alarming fact that this fatal disease could be contracted by children, either at birth through an infected mother or through a blood transfusion. The consequences, in addition to the expected fatality of the disease, could be deeply disturbing. When it became known that seventh grader Ryan White of Kokomo, Indiana, had contracted AIDS through a blood transfusion, he was locked out of his school in August 1985.

School officials did permit a special telephone line to be installed in the school so Ryan could take part in his classes from home. But neither Ryan nor his mother believed this was an adequate substitute for being there. Even though there was no possible way that someone could contract AIDS under ordinary conditions or casual contact, the fear was so great that many turned against Ryan White and other schoolchildren with AIDS.

THE MENTALLY ILL, BACK IN THE COMMUNITY

For many years, the only way of dealing with a person who was mentally ill was to put her or him in an institution. By 1955, the number of mentally ill persons who had been institutionalized had reached a peak of 560,000. By 1984, the number had dwindled to about 120,000. The reason? There were several, one being the development of medication to treat the symptoms of mental illness more effectively. For example, while there was as yet no medication that could cure schizophrenia and other forms of mental illness, medication had been developed to minimize or control such symptoms as hallucinations, delusions, and intense anxiety.

Another reason for the dramatic decrease in the number of institutionalized patients was a change in philosophy about treatment of the mentally ill. Caregivers now believed that treatment in the community, closer to home, family, and job, was better and cheaper than institutionalization. It was also more humane.

The rights of all patients, including those with mental illness, was another factor advanced by advocates of better treatment for the mentally ill. These advocates wanted to end such practices as commitment of people to hospitals without their consent, and to give patients the right to refuse treatment. They also wanted patients to receive treatment in the least restrictive environment possible.

New forms of funding made the new philosophy practical. With the enactment of Medicare, Medicaid, and supplemental security income, the states received welcome financial relief. Most of the money needed for the care and treatment of the severely and chronically mentally ill now came from the federal government.

ASPIRIN AND REYE'S SYNDROME

Aspirin is one of the most useful and easily obtainable drugs on the market. But a study in 1985 showed that when aspirin was used in treating certain common childhood diseases, it could be extremely harmful and potentially fatal. This turned out to be the case in a pilot study of the link between aspirin and Reye's syndrome. The study was released in January 1985, and by summer the first lawsuit was filed against a drug company by the parents of a child who had contracted Reye's syndrome.

Reye's syndrome is caused by a virus and can be fatal. Its symptoms may include vomiting, fever, convulsions, and coma. The pilot study showed that children who were given aspirin when they were suffering from flu or chicken pox were put at risk for developing Reye's syndrome.

THE RIGHT TO DIE

Karen Ann Quinlan lived in a small town in New Jersey. In 1975, when she was twenty-one, she went to a party, and after consuming several gin and tonics and a small quantity of tranquilizers, she passed out. When she stopped breathing, friends attempted mouth-to-mouth resuscitation. Then they took her, still unconscious, to the nearest hospital. Although Quinlan's breathing was restored, she never regained consciousness. She remained in this condition, called a coma, for ten years, kept alive by means of life-sustaining mechanical equipment.

Finally, her parents requested permission from the New Jersey Supreme Court to have the life-sustaining equipment withdrawn so Quinlan would be allowed to die. The court agreed when medical authorities testified that there was no reasonable possibility that she would ever recover. The court's decision laid the foundation for an important legal precedent in deciding similar issues in future cases. For a time, Quinlan continued to live by breathing on her own and by receiving food and antibiotics through a tube. When Karen Ann Quinlan died in June 1985, the cause of her death was attributed to respiratory failure following a series of lung infections.

DRUGS TO LOWER CHOLESTEROL

It was announced in 1987 that as many as twenty million Americans had cholesterol levels high enough to put them at risk for heart disease. Cholesterol is a chemical closely related to fats and an essential ingredient in the formation of cells and hormones. However, high levels of cholesterol in the blood can clog veins and arteries, slowing or blocking the flow of blood to the heart and causing heart problems. Clearly some form of drug was needed to help lower the cholesterol of people at risk. Before 1987, the only drug that had been approved by the U.S. Food and Drug Administration was cholestyramine, but it had serious drawbacks.

Two of the side effects were flatulence and bloating. Also, it came in the form of a powder that had to be mixed with a liquid and then swallowed. The resulting mixture was so gritty that some people said it was "like drinking Miami Beach." In 1987, a new drug was approved, lovastatin, that came in tablet form, making it easy to use. It was hailed as the first of a new class of cholesterol-lowering drugs, and it had none of the drawbacks of its predecessor.

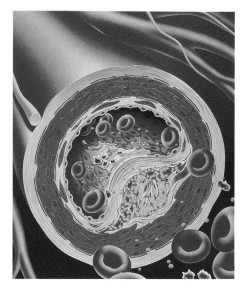

This illustration of the narrowing of an artery shows the artery cut through. The artery has been narrowed by the accumulation of cholesterol (yellow) beneath its inner wall (white).

THE DANGERS OF LYME DISEASE

Lyme, Connecticut, may not like the distinction, but an infectious form of arthritis that is potentially fatal has been named Lyme disease. The first cases of the disease were reported in the city of Lyme.

Lyme disease is caused by bacteria transmitted to humans by certain species of ticks carried by mice and deer. It starts with a rash, then the victim develops joint pains and flulike symptoms. These include chills, fever, headache, muscle aches, and a general feeling of ill health. Antibiotics usually clear up the symptoms if a patient is treated promptly. But Lyme disease can recur.

Medical observers pointed out that Lyme disease was the most common tick-borne illness in the United States, with cases reported in more than thirty states. By 1986, the number of cases reported had reached 5,000, and the number appeared to be doubling each year. Anyone living in an infected area was warned to take every precaution against tick bites. Health authorities sought to identify infected areas so that they could warn people to protect themselves.

DNA Fingerprinting

All forms of life—plant, animal, and human—are made up of tiny units called cells. A fully grown human has more than one hundred trillion cells. That's how tiny they are. Within each cell are chromosomes containing genes that determine each person's hereditary characteristics such as hair color, body size, shape and color of eyes, as well as intelligence, talents, and athletic ability.

The genes or genetic information are contained in a material known as deoxyribonucleic acid, referred to as DNA. DNA consists of four nucleotides: adenine, guanine, cytosine, and thymine. In a single human cell there may be six billion of these nucleotides. It is the number and arrangement of these nucleotides in each person's DNA that determine his or her genetic code.

The use of DNA to establish personal identity in lawsuits, including suits to identify the fathers of children, and in murder trials to prove the identity of murderers (as in the O. J. Simpson murder trial of the nineties) became firmly established in 1988.

The idea was developed by an Englishman, Alec Jeffreys, a geneticist at the University of Leicester. Several years before, he had been looking for genetic variations in DNA that showed that certain diseases in children had been inherited from one or both parents.

While doing this, Jeffreys began to wonder if variations in DNA patterns could also be used to identify people. A dramatic opportunity to test the

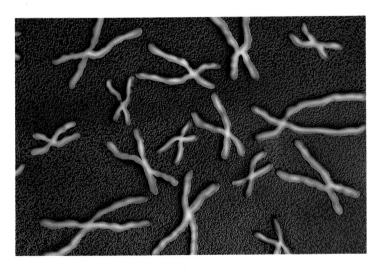

A color-enhanced micrograph— a photograph taken through a microscope—shows normal female chromosomes during cell division. The threadlike chromosomes are found in the cell nucleus and carry genetic information in the form of genes.

validity of this idea came in 1987 when two fifteen-year-old girls were found raped and strangled to death in the Leicester countryside. More than 5,000 men living in the area were given the DNA identification test as the police searched for the guilty person.

They found the murderer when they tested Colin Pitchfork. The DNA patterns in the blood sample taken from Pitchfork clearly matched the DNA patterns in the semen samples taken from the murder victims. The chance of two individuals having the same DNA patterns is extremely remote: only one in fifty billion. Because of this, authorities believed there was no reasonable doubt about Pitchfork's guilt. He was the only man who could have left the semen found on the murder victims.

A Patent for an Invention, But for a Mouse?

In April 1988, the U.S. Patent and Trademark Office awarded a patent to Harvard University for a strain of genetically engineered mice. For many years, scientists had been using mice in experiments designed to improve life for humans by finding cures for disease. Never before, however, had they felt it necessary to request a patent for the mice they were using.

Patents are something inventors need to protect their inventions from being stolen or copied by others without permission. Getting a patent for certain kinds of mice became important when recombinant DNA technology was introduced to the scientific world. Mice used in cancer experiments, for example, could be given an altered form of a normal gene that would make them unusually susceptible to cancer.

By the late 1980s, almost any kind of gene could be introduced to a wide variety of animals, making them models for many kinds of human disease. This led scientists to hope that new kinds of treatments, as well as cures, might be developed in the future.

Aspirin as an Anti-Heart Attack Drug

In 1988, manufacturers of aspirin and the public at large were elated with the medical report that proposed that aspirin could lessen the chances of a heart attack. This possibility was indicated in a five-year study of 22,000 healthy physicians over age forty. The study was conducted by Charles Hennekens and his associates at Harvard Medical School. They divided the group of physicians into two groups: those who were given aspirin and those who were given a placebo, a tablet with no medical value.

Those physicians who took one 325-milligram aspirin tablet every other day, the study showed, had a greatly reduced incidence of first heart attacks, compared to those who had not been given the aspirin therapy. There were 104 heart attacks in the aspirin-taking group, compared to 189 in the nonaspirin or placebo group.

Most heart attacks happen when blood clots form in arteries leading to the heart, cutting off the heart's blood supply and, if not treated in time, destroying heart tissue. Aspirin reduces the aggregation, or clumping, of platelets in the blood, and in this way prevents blood clots from forming.

However, there is also a major disadvantage in aspirin therapy. The overuse of aspirin can lead to internal bleeding or hemorrhaging, which can put a person at risk of hemorrhagic stroke. Like a heart attack, strokes can be fatal as well as physically damaging. Because of this and other possible side effects, caution was advised, including consultation with a physician, before using aspirin to protect against heart attacks.

LOCATING THE CYSTIC FIBROSIS GENE

Progress continued to be made in genetics and gene therapy. A highlight in 1989 was the identification of the gene that causes cystic fibrosis. Two teams of scientists shared in the discovery, Lap-Chee Tsui and John Riordan of the Hospital for Sick Children in Toronto, Canada, and Francis Collins and his colleagues at the Howard Hughes Medical Institute at the University of Michigan in Ann Arbor. The studies showed that the protein controlled by the cystic fibrosis gene apparently regulates the movement of vital substances across cell membranes.

When the protein is abnormal, this leads to the development of the thick, sticky mucus that clogs the lungs and digestive systems of those afflicted with cystic fibrosis. The discovery of the cystic fibrosis gene led to optimism that in time it might be possible to treat the disorder successfully by supplying sufferers with the protein they lacked. It also might be possible in the future to correct or replace defective proteins by means of gene therapy, that is, by replacing abnormal genes with normal ones.

3

COMPUTERS

Development of the computer as a major resource in science and business as well as for personal use clearly dominated the decade of the 1980s. The potential of the computer to "think"—to show cause, effect, and solution—was remarkable. The first use of computer technology in automobiles brought the bar chart fuel gauge, the digital speedometer, and a message center that could alert drivers to mechanical problems.

Computers were also at the center of an information explosion with the introduction of CD-ROM technology. Laser-based like compact disc music recordings, CD-ROM was a boon to scientific researchers and writers. It allowed thousands of pages of printed information to be made available on just one CD-ROM disc.

COMPUTER GEAR ON AUTOMOBILES

One of the major breakthroughs in 1980 was the installation of computer devices on automobiles. The Lincoln Mark VI, for instance, had three micro-computers on its dashboard. One was a bar chart fuel gauge, the second was a digital speedometer, and the third was a message center. The message center had the amazing ability to spell out information about thirty-six different mechanical conditions. During a trip, it could also keep the driver posted on how many miles away a particular destination happened to be.

Two Cadillac models, the Seville and the Eldorado, used a computer chip to show fuel consumption. General Motors announced that in the next year, 1981, it would include a computerized emission control system on every one of its cars.

Ford and Chrysler also said they would be installing computer devices on their models. It was predicted that by 1983 American carmakers would be

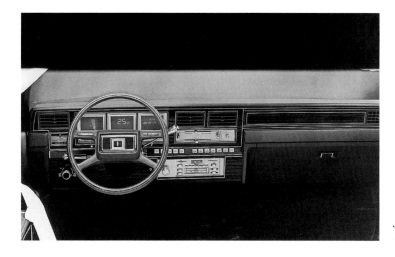

The Lincoln Mark VI, with three dashboard micro-computers, was in the forefront of automotive design in the early 1980s.

providing computers that talked, so they could tell owners what was wrong with their cars when they malfunctioned. But by then this remained a prediction still to be realized.

COMPUTER WORKSTATIONS

In 1981, one of the giants of the computer industry, IBM Corporation, introduced its first personal computer system. A competing firm, Xerox Corporation, introduced a personal computer of its own, the Star 8010, but this one was designed for use in offices as a workstation. It was called "the office of the future."

By the mid-1980s, it was expected that office automation systems, designed to improve the productivity of workers, would make it possible for data processing, word processing, electronic mail, and voice and video applications to operate off the same device.

COMPUTER MICE

Developments continued in the computer industry. One of the most unusual was the introduction in 1983 of a handheld device called a mouse because of its small, rounded shape and the long, slim, flexible cord that connected it to an electrical socket in the computer. The mouse could be used in place of the computer keyboard for many basic operations, providing a welcome convenience for those who used computers at work or at home.

Another development that made computers easier to operate was a touch-sensitive display screen, which made it possible for some operations to be done by touching the screen instead of using the keyboard or mouse. Advances were also made in the development of voice recognition. Computer developers hoped that eventually computer users would be able to interact with the computer by giving it commands by voice, in other words by actually *telling* it what to do.

COMPUTERS THAT "THINK"

By 1984, computer manufacturers in both Japan and the United States had made good on promises to give computers the ability to think for themselves. This "artificial intelligence" capability included the ability of the computer to understand and follow spoken commands, such as "Get the payroll file." This eliminated the need for a computer operator to use his or her mouse or the keyboard in a much more complicated process to get the same results: show the wanted file on the monitor screen.

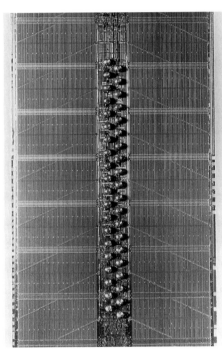

Computers became more powerful in 1984 through the widespread commercial use of new 256-kilobit memory chips. One kilobit is equal to 1,024 bits. A bit is the smallest increment of usable computer data. The new chips were four times more powerful than the former memory chips, whose capability was only 64-kilobit memory storage.

The 256-kilobit memory chip, manufactured by IBM

CD-ROM: THE INFORMATION EXPLOSION

One of the most revolutionary computer advances of the decade occurred in 1986. Called compact disc read-only memory, or CD-ROM, this new development made it possible for books stored on a computer disk to come alive with sound and animated pictures. Maps could be explored down to the street level. Thousands of photos could be stored in minuscule space. Like the compact disc music recordings that also appeared for the first time in 1986, CD-ROM technology was made possible by using a laser beam to record information on a plastic disk 4.75 inches (12 centimeters) in diameter. CD-ROM, however, was played back into a personal computer and a special player rather than into a sound system.

The results were astonishing. For instance, just one CD-ROM disk could store all of the information contained in approximately 1,200 single-sided floppy disks or 270,000 pages of printed information. Another advantage of the CD-ROM was that data contained on a disk could be searched for just by typing one key word.

Medical researchers could type the word *cancer* on their computer keyboards and get a list of all the articles on the disk they were using that contained the word *cancer*. A parallel development was CD-I, or Compact Disc Interactive, which made it possible for the CD-ROM disk to store sound and pictures as well as text. The Compact Disc Interactive also permitted quick and easy movement from CD-ROM to CD-I.

Computers That Talk to One Another

Among the most important concerns of computer manufacturers in 1988 was the need for standardization and intercomputer communication. At a conference in Baltimore, Maryland, fifty computer manufacturers from around the world met to demonstrate how their computers could communicate with one another. This was accomplished through the use of a standard set of communications rules called Open Systems Interconnection (OSI). At the demonstration in Baltimore, 310 computers communicated with one another. The need for different computers to communicate with one another became increasingly important as more and more industries computerized their operations.

Viruses Infect Computers

The first known instance of a "virus" infecting a computer happened on March 2, 1988. Macintosh II computers that were using new software for drawing pictures were suddenly interrupted by a message calling for world peace. This message was only briefly irritating to the Macintosh users because it disappeared in a few seconds. But when the virus "infected" other computers, it became a major problem because it accidentally destroyed their data.

It was not long before computer viruses became epidemic. Some were simple, brief interruptions, like the virus that demanded, "I want cookie!" However, the interruption could only be ended with the correct response, which was "Oreo." Sometimes other viruses would wait until all of the computer user's software programs had become infected. Then the viruses would erase the hard disk, destroying all the data in the computer's memory.

The most common method of entry for computer viruses was through noncommercial computer programs. This was the kind of software either given away or sold at low cost at group meetings for computer users or made available through electronic bulletin boards. Bulletin boards served as exchanges for computer programs or software. In fact, a bulletin board had been the source of the first computer virus.

HOW VIRUSES INFECT COMPUTERS

Before methods of preventing viruses from infecting computers were developed in the 1990s, the computer virus was a major threat to the "health" of the computers used in business and at home. Sometimes the virus was relatively harmless, with no ill will intended, but a virus could also be totally destructive.

A computer virus is a program or set of instructions that someone puts on a floppy disk that is either intended to be used with a computer or introduced to other computers when computer users are communicating over telephone lines or data networks. Stealthily, without calling attention to itself, the virus copies itself into the operating systems of other computers. In this way, it can infect many thousands of computers.

In 1988, a relatively benign example of a computer virus was created by *Mac Mag*, a magazine for computer hobbyists. It turned up in a graphics program called Freehand, developed for Macintosh computers. The virus carried a message to be flashed on infected computer screens on March 2. The message said, "Richard Brandow, publisher of Mac Mag, and its entire staff would like to take this opportunity to convey their universal message of peace to all Macintosh users around the world." It was estimated that this particular virus ultimately infected several hundred thousand Macintosh computers.

Like this virus, other viruses might carry instructions to be set off only on a certain date or after making a certain number of copies of themselves. But viruses could also be programmed to be as destructive as carrying instructions for the infected computer to destroy all the information it had stored in it, instantly destroying months or years of valuable work.

To prevent viruses from infecting computers, it was recommended that business users be banned from using anything other than commercial software. Those who used personal computers at home were advised never to copy a noncommercial program onto a hard disk without testing it first. They were also advised to use one or more of the new computer protective devices then becoming available. By 1991, these included the Norton Antivirus, manufactured by Symantec Corporation, and Hyperaccess/5, produced by Hilgraeve, Inc. The Norton Antivirus scanned a user's disk for known viruses and removed them. It also protected the computer from subsequent attacks.

For those peple who "downloaded" or started their computers from another computer via telephone lines, Hyperaccess/5 filtered out all known viruses from the incoming data before they could infect the user's machine.

4

TECHNOLOGY

Technology in the 1980s grappled with energy and environmental problems. Buildings were designed with energy saving in mind, and so were bridges and tunnels, including the projected tunnel in the English Channel that would provide a direct rail link between Great Britain and France, and therefore all of Europe.

DESIGNING BUILDINGS THAT SAVE ENERGY

One of the important decisions President Jimmy Carter made in his last year in office, 1980, was to submit a proposal to Congress for tax incentives encouraging the use of passive solar heating and cooling in both houses and nonresidential buildings. Any company that constructed such a house or building would qualify for a tax credit. Incentives for constructing energy-saving buildings were also introduced in Great Britain and other European countries.

When the United States architectural firm of Davis, Brody and Associates designed a new biochemistry laboratory for Princeton University in New Jersey, it incorporated four distinct elevations. Each was designed to respond to a different environmental factor.

Large areas of glass were used in the east and west walls to meet the requirements for maximum daylight. Because the intensity of the sun was greatest on the south wall, the glassed-in areas there were small. The wall that faced north, where most of the winter cold would come from, was nearly without any glass at all.

Designers of other buildings made economical use of energy by letting more of the sun and its warmth into their buildings. They accomplished this through such features as atriums, glass-enclosed courts, skylights, window patterns, and other sun control devices.

CENTENNIAL OF THE ELECTRIC POWER INDUSTRY

The year 1981 marked the hundredth anniversary of the first use of electric power in home and industry. It was in 1881 that chemist Joseph Swan in England began the manufacture of filament lamps. America's Thomas Edison, the inventor of the "Edison effect," which become the basis for the electron tube, was building his first two power stations, one in New York City and the other in London, England, in 1881.

That same year, the first public supply of electricity was switched on in a small English town called Godalming. The British House of Commons, a factory in New York City, and ships, trains, and theater stages were also lit by electricity.

One of the early lamps made by Swan produced two lumens of light intensity per watt of electric power. A hundred years later, ninety lumens per watt had been

Thomas Edison stands beside the dynamo that generated the energy for the first commercial electric light.

OLYMPICS OF MATH

In July 1981, for the first time in the Western Hemisphere, the International Mathematical Olympiad was held in Washington, D.C. This was the twenty-second annual event, and it drew 185 high-school students from twenty-seven countries. For the second time in five years, the United States team won first place. But it was not an easy win. A close second, only two points behind, was the team from West Germany. The two-day contest consisted of six complex problems, with three to be completed each day within a four-and-a-half-hour period. Four members of the United States team had perfect scores. This was the first time this had been achieved by any team.

achieved for white light sources. There was also a renewed interest in developing automobiles and other road vehicles that could be powered by electricity. This would conserve energy by reducing the amount of gas and oil consumed. It would also reduce the amount of air pollution caused by the burning of those fuel sources.

In 1981, the first electric vehicle made under the sponsorship of the U.S. Department of Energy was exhibited in London. One observer estimated that if electric vehicles proved practical, there could be thirty-four million such vehicles on the road in the United States within the next twenty years.

A Technological Marvel: Rubik's Cube

Technology can take many forms, and in 1981 one of the marvels of the year was a toy designed by a Hungarian professor, Erno Rubik. Called Rubik's Cube, the toy was an intriguing puzzle that piqued the interest and fascination of adults as well as children. Many millions were sold all over the world.

Rubik's Cube was a puzzle in the shape of a large cube, made up of twenty-seven smaller cubes. All of the smaller cubes were the same size, but they were of various colors. Each layer of nine smaller cubes could be rotated. The object of the puzzle was to restore each face of the cube to a single color after the colors had been mixed up by rotation of the various layers.

Capitalizing on the Rubik's Cube craze, a thirteen-year-old boy from London, England, Patrick Bossert, who solved the puzzle, wrote a 112-page book entitled *You Can Do the Cube*. The book sold 750,000 copies in Great Britain and other European countries. It also brought the young author distinction in the United States. He became the youngest author ever to have a book on the best-seller list of the *New York Times*.

Using Satellites to Save Lives

A young Belgian race car driver had an accident in a remote section of Somalia, Africa, and might have died had his exact position not been identified by search-and-rescue satellites. There were no ground communications or medical facilities nearby to assist him.

Alerted to the emergency, two search-and-rescue satellites, *NOAA 9* of the United States and *Cospos 1* of the Soviet Union, fixed his position and notified authorities, who hastened to the scene of the accident. They transported the injured man by air to a hospital in Brussels, Belgium, where he later recovered. By the end of May 1985, more than 400 lives had been saved by the network of three Soviet and two U.S. search-and-rescue satellites.

Search-and-rescue satellites continued to play critical roles in saving humans from danger and also in protecting military personnel. Another important development in this type of satellite was a technology called remote sensing. In 1994, this technology was being used to identify areas infested with the deer tick, an insect that carries the Lyme disease bacteria, which, as stated earlier, can cause chronic heart disease and other health problems if not treated promptly with antibiotics.

A Landsat satellite equipped with remote sensing devices was positioned 435 miles (700 kilometers) above the earth and used its electronic scanner to study the landscape in Westchester County, New York. Westchester has one of the highest rates of Lyme disease in the United States. The satellite compared vegetation patterns with data about dogs known to carry the Lyme disease bacteria. Deer tick populations are known to be attracted to lawns that have shady trees and high ornamental shrubs, and that are located close to densely wooded areas. All of this information was fed into a computer, which produced a color-coded map showing areas most likely to contain deer tick populations.

TITANIC MYSTERY SOLVED

One of the great tragedies of the early twentieth century occurred on April 15, 1912, when the ocean liner *Titanic* collided with an iceberg about 560 miles (900 kilometers) south of Newfoundland and sank to the bottom of the ocean. It was not until seventy-three years later, on September 1, 1985, that the wreck was located. This was made possible by an underwater search vehicle called *Argo*.

The *Argo* was able to transmit images of the remains of the *Titanic*, showing a boiler with three fire doors, to the United States research vessel *Knorr*. About the size of a large automobile, the *Argo* had powerful lights and sensitive video cameras. The wreck of the *Titanic* lay at a depth of 13,100 feet (3,990 meters). Its hull had been broken in two, and debris from the wreck was spread over a huge area hundreds of yards long.

The disastrous sinking of the British luxury liner Titanic *claimed 1,517 lives. There were 711 survivors.*

DR. ROBERT D. BALLARD: DISCOVERER OF THE *TITANIC*

Robert Duane Ballard was born on June 30, 1942, in Wichita, Kansas. After receiving degrees in chemistry and geology at the University of California in Santa Barbara, he joined the U.S. Navy. Because of his background in science, he was made liaison officer at the Office of Naval Research at the Woods Hole, Massachusetts, Oceanographic Institution. Three years later, he left the navy to become a civilian researcher, but he remained at Woods Hole. At the time of the *Titanic* discovery, he was head of the institution's Deep Submergence Laboratory.

Dr. Ballard and his team of underwater researchers found the *Titanic* on the edge of a submarine canyon seventy-three years after it had plunged to the bottom of the ocean. It had lost its stern and two of its four smokestacks, but otherwise its preservation was remarkable. *Argo* took more than 12,000 color photos of the wreck.

It was not until 1993, however, that some of the *Titanic's* treasures were brought to land. These included fine china, three ship's whistles—each of which weighed 800 pounds (360 kilograms)—spittoons, and hundreds of other artifacts.

By then, Dr. Ballard had been involved in several other undersea discoveries, including the location of the German battleship *Bismarc58*, sunk during World War II. In 1993, he supervised the wiring of the ocean liner *Lusitania*, sunk during World War I, with robot cameras. The cameras roved about inside the sunken liner, relaying images by cable to museums on land.

ROBOTS IMITATING HUMANS

By 1981, the men and women involved in designing robots for use in industry had become experts in creating robots that could be programmed to repeat actions as directed. For example, robots that had the ability to assemble parts were being used in plants that manufactured small electric and electronic appliances, such as videotape recorders, copiers, and electric fans. By 1983, inventors were concentrating on designing robots that would be capable of recognition and judgment.

It was predicted that future robots would be equipped with sensors, giving them the added powers of sight and touch. They would therefore be able to identify objects and hold both soft and hard materials in their hands. Robots could also be used for inspection and maintenance jobs.

Using robots in this way at nuclear power stations, for instance, meant they would be able to perform tasks that are potentially hazardous for human beings. For this type of job, robots would be equipped with the "eyes" of a television camera and would have sensors that could record temperature and radiation measurements. They would also have multijointed arms capable of performing complicated operations.

A TUNNEL TO LINK ENGLAND AND FRANCE

One of the stellar events of 1986 was the announcement that Great Britain and France had agreed to cooperate in a joint project to build an underwater tunnel across the English Channel. This would create a permanent link between the two countries. A tunnel railway system would move passengers and freight, with entrance and exit points at Cheriton, England, and Frethun, France.

An Anglo-French construction and banking group was given the contract to build the project, to be known as Eurotunnel, at a cost of nearly $3.8 billion. It was expected to open to rail traffic in 1993. Up to 4,000 vehicles an hour would be carried in each direction by means of shuttle trains built especially for this purpose. Conventional trains would also be able to use the tunnel to make the journey between the two countries. In this way, British passenger and freight networks would be directly connected with the European system.

Workers congratulate each other after breaking through the last of the rock separating the two sides of the Eurotunnel, nicknamed the Chunnel.

All of Eurotunnel's goals were achieved when the tunnel opened for commercial traffic in October 1994. The crossing from Great Britain to France took thirty-five minutes on a specially designed train that sped along at 90 miles (145 kilometers) per hour. The opening of the underwater tunnel provided the first physical link between Great Britain and France since the time when the two landmasses were joined during the Ice Age, 10,000 years ago. The Eurotunnel, the longest submarine tunnel in the world, was the largest civil engineering project ever undertaken by private business firms.

New York to Tokyo in Two and a Half Hours

Opportunities to increase the speed of air travel continued to interest aircraft manufacturers during the 1980s. The Concorde supersonic aircraft used by

British Airways on transatlantic routes had managed to keep the public interested in high-speed air travel in spite of the expense involved. High-speed travel appealed to businesspeople in particular, as they sought to cut down the number of hours they spent in the air instead of in the office.

With this in mind, in 1986 McDonnell Douglas came up with a new aircraft design, called the Orient Express, that would far exceed the Concorde in both speed and passenger capacity. With room for 300 passengers, it would be able to cruise at an altitude of 99,000 feet (30,175 meters). It had a maximum speed that was five times the speed of sound, or 2,976 miles (4,800 kilometers) per hour. And it would cover a distance of approximately 7,440 miles (12,000 kilometers) without the need for refueling. By contrast, the Concorde carried 128 passengers at a top speed of 1,333 miles (2,150 kilometers) per hour at a maximum distance of 3,038 miles (4,900 kilometers).

The time factor was the most impressive statistic of all. McDonnell Douglas's Orient Express could reduce the flight time from New York to Tokyo from fourteen hours to only two and a half hours.

Although McDonnell Douglas's plans for the Orient Express never advanced to production of the plane, the company continued to be a contender in the competition to produce supersonic aircraft (aircraft that travels faster than the speed of sound). In 1994, McDonnell Douglas and the Boeing Company were selected by NASA (National Aeronautics and Space Administration) to lead a team to develop technologies for the next generation of supersonic transport aircraft. They were beneficiaries of an $880 million contract from NASA for an eight-year segment of its high-speed research program.

5

SPACE

One of the peaks of space exploration in the 1980s was the opportunity to take the first really close look at Halley's comet, which passes the earth only once every seventy-six years. The last time the comet had appeared was in 1910. This time, spacecraft from the United States, the Soviet Union, Japan, and the European Space Agency were well prepared to study and record their observations of the phenomenon. The most sensational observations were made by the European Space Agency spacecraft *Giotto*, which flew into Halley's comet's tail and behind the nucleus, taking more than 2,000 photos.

Another grand achievement was the Soviet Union's success in establishing a permanent orbiting space station. This became the focus of many space missions and numerous tests of human endurance in outer space. By decade's end, the record of 362 days in space had been set by the Soviets.

The United States was not without its achievements, among them close observations of Venus, Jupiter, Saturn, Uranus, and Neptune. There were also commercial achievements in outer space, such as the launching of communications satellites, and products developed for use in space put to good use on earth.

The United States also sent its first woman into space, Sally Ride. As a mission specialist aboard the *Challenger*, she performed scientific assignments and served as flight engineer.

RUSSIANS SPEND 185 DAYS IN SPACE

The Russians scored a major achievement in 1980 when they sent a team of cosmonauts to *Salyut 6* space station, where they spent a record-setting 185 days before returning to earth on October 11. It was the first time that Leonid Popov had been in space. But his partner, Valeri Ryumin, had been in space twice before, for 2 days in 1977 and for 175 days in 1979. This gave Ryumin a cumulative total of 362 days in space, only 3 days short of one full year's experience in living and working in outer space.

When they were examined on their return to earth, neither cosmonaut showed any signs of disability. Both men had gained weight, and each had grown an inch, but that was a temporary gain, soon lost as they readjusted to earth's gravity.

While aboard *Salyut 6*, the cosmonauts had performed several scientific experiments. In one experiment, they grew various kinds of crystals in the weightless environment. This was done in an attempt to produce better material for semiconductors, used in electricity as conductors and insulators, and to improve the production of polyurethane foam structures. The men also studied the production and effect of interferon in human cells. By the time the mission had ended, the Soviets had spent 45,564 hours in space. This was more than twice as much as the United States, whose total in 1980 was just 22,494 hours.

UNITED STATES SPACE PROBE ON VENUS

In 1978, the United States had sent a space probe, *Pioneer-Venus*, to Venus, and in 1980 it continued to transmit data to earth. This data helped convince scientists that Venus's extremely hot surface, 900°F (482°C), was caused by an atmospheric greenhouse effect. When radiation from the sun hits the planet, it is trapped by gases in the planet's atmosphere. It is not reflected back into space.

There were also some judgments made about Venus's evolution. When the solar system was formed, Venus's atmosphere received much higher quantities of certain elements from

Launched in 1978, the Pioneer-Venus *probe transmitted data for almost fourteen years. This false-color image of Venus was created from information gathered by* Pioneer-Venus.

the sun than earth did. Among the gases found on Venus were argon-36, krypton, and xenon.

The *Pioneer-Venus* probe continued to transmit data to earth until 1992, when its thrusters failed to fire, causing it to plummet through Venus's atmosphere and burn up in the intense heat. It was the first American spacecraft to circle Venus, and over the years it had mapped more than 90 percent of the planet's surface.

A COMET HITS THE SUN

In one of the most remarkable astronomical events of the year 1981, scientists reported that a comet had hit the sun. This event actually occurred in 1979, but it was not seen by any ground-based observatory. It was detected by a U.S. Air Force satellite that had been launched in February of 1979. However, it was not until late 1981 and 1982 that reports confirmed the event. It was documented by a device aboard the satellite called a coronagraph. This device blots out the intense radiation from the sun except for the corona that surrounds it. It also takes photographs at ten-minute intervals.

A series of photographs by the coronagraph revealed a comet on a straight path to the sun, trailing a tail typical of comets. When the comet hit the sun, it disappeared from view, suggesting it may have evaporated on contact due to the sun's intense radiation.

TEENAGER'S INSECT STUDY PERFORMED IN SPACE

When the United States space shuttle orbiter *Columbia* lifted off on March 22, 1982, it carried with it an insect study experiment developed by eighteen-year-old Todd E. Nelson, a senior at Southland High School in Adams, Minnesota. The orbiter was manned by astronauts Jack R. Lousma and C. Gordon Fullerton. Their mission lasted eight days before they returned to earth, landing March 29 at the White Sands Missile Range in New Mexico.

Todd Nelson was one of ten finalists in the first national competition for students to design experiments for a space shuttle mission. The competition was developed by NASA and the National Science Teachers Association. Each entry accepted is sponsored by a business firm. Todd's sponsor was the

Avionics Division of Honeywell, Inc., in Minneapolis, which has provided navigational aids for the shuttle program.

Two species of insects were chosen: the velvet bean caterpillar moth and the honeybee drone, which exhibit great differences in ratio of body mass to wing area. Several moths and honeybees were put in separate canisters and placed in middeck in the shuttle's living area. When the insects emerged from the canisters into a cage, an astronaut studied and photographed their behavior in a weightless environment as the space shuttle orbited the earth.

On future flights, it was expected that experiments would include those developed by industry, individuals, schools, and other organizations, the number determined in part by space available aboard the orbiter.

Soviet Probes on Venus

More information about earth's closest neighbor, Venus, became available in 1982, when the Soviet Union's space probe, *Venera 13*, landed there on March 1. The landing site was a plain to the east of the Phoebe region in the Beta area. It took only sixty-two minutes for the space probe to travel through the planet's thick atmosphere.

For two hours and seven minutes, *Venera 13* transmitted data to scientists in the Soviet Union. This included chemical analyses of the soil and color photographs of the surface. The ground temperature was found to be 854.6°F (457°C). Elements in the soil included magnesium, silicon, aluminum, sodium, potassium, titanium, manganese, and iron. The rocks were the color of rust, and the sky was orange and reddish brown. At its surface, the atmospheric pressure on Venus was eighty-nine times greater than it is on earth.

Spin-offs From Space Exploration

Over the years, the exploration of space by the United States and other nations has produced a bountiful number of technological developments. Some were developed out of necessity, and some were innovations meant to increase the success and expand the potential worth of later space missions. By 1983, for example, the heat shield on United States spacecraft was made of more than 30,000 ceramic tiles. This made it possible for spacecraft to withstand the extremely high temperatures and powerful forces of air involved in blasting off into outer space.

Improvements continued to be made in the machinery to increase a spacecraft's power and reliability. The computer systems in United States spacecraft were so sophisticated in 1983 that they could almost operate a space shuttle on their own, without any human intervention, once they were programmed for a particular mission.

Space suits, life-support systems, and a small rocket backpack, called a manned maneuvering unit, were developed to allow astronauts to travel short distances through space between the shuttle and nearby objects. An important spin-off of the rocket backpack was developed by Essex Corporation for underwater use in special pools where astronauts could practice

---

SALLY RIDE, FIRST UNITED STATES WOMAN IN SPACE

The space shuttle *Challenger* had already chalked up a number of "firsts," but its June 18, 1983, flight was particularly memorable. Not only did it carry the largest crew ever launched into space at the same time, it had Sally Ride aboard, the first United States woman in space. Only two other women had preceded her, both from the Soviet Union.

A mission specialist on the *Challenger*, Ride performed a number of scientific assignments and also served as flight engineer.

Sally Ride

The mission lasted six days, and during that period, assisted by other crew members, she deployed two communications satellites. Ride also released and retrieved a satellite using the shuttle's mechanical arm. This was equipment that she had helped to design. Chalk up yet another first for *Challenger*!

Sally Ride was thirty-two when she became the first United States woman in space. She was born in Encino, California, and loved sports, becoming especially successful in tennis. This resulted in the offer of a partial scholarship to a girls' preparatory school in Los Angeles. This is when she became interested in science.

Ride went on to college, majoring in physics at Swarthmore College in Pennsylvania. She continued her studies at Stanford University, where she received a doctorate in astrophysics in 1978. A year before she graduated, she had applied to NASA, which was recruiting young scientists.

In 1978, Sally Ride was one of six women and twenty-nine men selected by NASA. She received training at the Johnson Space Center in Houston, Texas, and on the second and third space shuttle flights she was the capsule communicator. This meant she was the person on the ground who talked to astronauts in flight in outer space. By 1983, she had become an astronaut herself.

working in weightless conditions. The same device was considered by off-shore oil companies. The rocket backpack would increase the endurance and working abilities of divers.

A giant mechanical arm, called a remote manipulator system, was developed to allow astronauts to perform tasks outside the spacecraft without leaving the spacecraft's cabin. The developer of the mechanical arm, Spar Aerospace of Canada, was exploring the possibility of a variation of the device that could be mounted on wheelchairs for use by handicapped persons, such as quadriplegics, who were unable to use their arms.

PIONEER 10 LEAVES THE SOLAR SYSTEM

For ten years, since its launch in 1972, the United States space probe *Pioneer 10* had been traveling through the solar system, continuously transmitting data back to scientists on earth. Finally, on June 13, 1983, it became the first man-made object to leave the known limits of the solar system. Some scientists believed life-forms might exist on other planets, life-forms sometimes referred to as extraterrestrials. If they didn't exist on some planet in earth's solar system, then perhaps extraterrestrials were living on a planet in some other system in outer space.

With the possibility in mind that *Pioneer 10* might land on a planet that was home to extraterrestrials or might be captured by them, the spacecraft carried a plaque aboard that had been designed by astronomer Carl Sagan. Among other things, it depicted a man and a woman and the solar system, with planet earth indicated as the origin of the space probe.

NASA hoped to be able to continue tracking *Pioneer 10* for another ten years. Equipped with a radioactive power supply, its electric power was expected to last for another twenty years, or until 2003. In 1991, *Pioneer 10* was more than 4 billion miles (6.5 billion kilometers) from earth and still sending data, almost twenty years after it had been launched. By 1993, the space probe was expected to be 5 billion miles (8 billion kilometers) from earth.

PROBES OF MARS AND HALLEY'S COMET

Included in NASA's budget for 1985 was a request for funding for a probe to be sent to the planet Mars. The *Mars* orbiter would provide data on climate as well as on the surface chemistry of the planet. An earlier probe by the *Viking* orbiter, launched in 1976, encouraged scientists to believe they could determine when water had produced the deep canyons that exist on Mars. They also hoped to have answers to questions about whether or not Mars could ever have sustained some form of life. A space probe named the *Mars Observer* was launched on September 25, 1992. It was NASA's first mission to the "red planet" since the 1970s, when the *Viking* landers were sent to Mars.

NASA had also made plans in 1984 to change the position of the *Pioneer* probe, then in orbit about Venus, so it could be used to observe Halley's comet in early 1986. That's when the comet would be at perihelion, or its closest point to the sun. The probe was equipped with an ultraviolet spectrometer that could be used to study the gases and dust emanating from the comet. *Pioneer* was expected to observe Halley's comet for a period of six to eight weeks, continuously transmitting its findings to scientists on earth.

CONSTRUCTION CREWS IN SPACE

November 29, 1985, marked a banner day in outer space for the United States. It was the first time American astronauts practiced construction techniques in outer space, techniques that would be used to build future space stations. While aboard the space shuttle *Atlantis*, the two-man team of Air Force Major Jerry Ross and Army Lieutenant Colonel Sherwood Spring worked with aluminum tubes and end connectors as they assembled and disassembled various structures.

On November 29, Ross and Spring spent five and a half hours at work, which left them unusually tired. They repeated the exercise two days later, this time spending almost seven hours at their task. The men accomplished their objectives but once again complained of fatigue. This suggested that working in outer space, in cumbersome space suits and in zero gravity, required more effort and endurance than the same type of work in the same time span on earth.

Completing other assignments on the *Atlantis* mission, the crew launched three communications satellites. One was a *SATCOM KU-2* launched for RCA American Communications, Inc. The other two were launched for foreign countries: *Morelos-B*, a Mexican communications satellite, and *Aussat-2*, Australia's communications satellite.

A TEACHER'S MISSION ENDS IN TRAGEDY

Sharon Christa McAuliffe, a teacher from Concord, New Hampshire, was the winner of a national competition to be the first teacher sent to outer space. Assigned to the crew of the space shuttle *Challenger*, she would conduct at least two lessons to be broadcast while the spaceship was in orbit. When it returned to earth, McAuliffe would spend the following nine months lecturing students across the United States. The announced goal of her mission was to highlight the importance of teachers as well as to interest students in high-technology careers, such as those offered by the United States space program.

Sadly, none of this happened. On the morning of January 28, 1986, soon after the space shuttle *Challenger* was launched at the Kennedy Space Center in Florida, it exploded. All aboard were killed. An investigation into the cause of the tragedy pointed to a faulty seal in one of the shuttle's two solid rocket boosters as the physical cause of the accident. NASA immediately ordered work to begin on a redesigned booster to use for future launches. In July, NASA announced that the shuttle program would not be ready to resume launchings until 1988. Shuttle launches did not actually resume, however, until 1989.

Christa McAuliffe, a high school social studies teacher, was chosen from more than 11,000 applicants to be part of the Challenger *mission.*

CATCHING UP WITH THE SOVIETS

Contrasted with the condition and objectives of the United States space program in 1986, the achievements of the Soviet Union were impressive. Not only had they completed a dual mission to Venus and Halley's comet, they had also launched a permanent space station, *Mir*, and were planning robot expeditions to Mars and Venus.

In 1985, United States President Ronald Reagan had appointed a commission headed by Thomas Paine, a former NASA administrator. The commission's objective was to come up with new goals for the United States space program. A year later, the announced goals included launching a United States space station in the 1990s and construction of a base on the moon in the early years of the twenty-first century. A third goal was an outpost on Mars that could be permanently occupied by 2035. NASA subsequently announced that construction of the space station would begin in 1993.

An International Space Station

By 1995, with approval still pending from Congress, the plans for a United States space station had evolved into a broader plan that would include Europe, Japan, Canada, and Russia as partners in an International Space Station. The cost to United States taxpayers would be $43 billion, including $11 billion that already had been spent on design studies by 1994.

It was estimated that eighty-five launchings of gear and astronauts would be needed to assemble and outfit the station. Space shuttle flights for this purpose were scheduled to begin in late 1997 and end in 2002. Plans called for an international crew of six astronauts to operate the space station. They would study planet earth, the heavens, and human reactions to weightlessness. This would be in preparation for long journeys to Mars and other planets.

Here Comes Halley!

Two astronomers, David Jewitt and G. Edward Danielson, were able to identify Halley's comet using the 200-inch (500-centimeter) Hale telescope on Mount Palomar near Escondido, California. At that time, in 1982, the comet was just beginning its approach toward earth. It was about 1 billion miles (1.6 billion kilometers) from earth and about one hundred million times too dim to be seen by the unaided eye. Halley's comet was expected to cross the earth's path in 1986. Without the aid of telescopes, it is only visible in earth's sky once every seventy-six years.

The scientists estimated Halley's comet would make its closest approach to the sun on February 9, 1986. Several countries announced plans to launch spacecraft to take photos and record observations of the comet. The Soviet Union was the first country to do this, launching two spacecraft in 1984, *Vega 1* and *Vega 2*. They would cross the comet's path on March 6 and 9, 1986. In 1985, Japan launched two spacecraft. The European Space Agency launched a space probe named *Giotto*, which would pass within 370 miles (592 kilometers) of the comet's nucleus and provide the first pictures of how a comet looks at that distance. The United States planned to view Halley's comet from a space shuttle orbiter. Observations were also made by the *Pioneer-Venus* orbiter. Because of its position, it was able to observe Halley's comet at its closest approach to the sun.

THE YIELD FROM HALLEY'S COMET

When Halley's comet crossed earth's orbit in March 1986, it was disappointing visually, nothing like the dazzling apparition it had been in 1910, when the earth passed through the comet's tail. That caused panic around the world. But this time, the scientific yields were bountiful. Scientists were able to take their first look at what some had characterized as "the icy leftovers from the birth of the solar system." Astronomer Fred Whipple had described comets as "dirty snowballs." The close looks taken at Halley's comet in 1986 showed the comet to be "dirtier" even than Whipple and other early astronomers had imagined.

The closest observations were made by the European Space Agency's spacecraft *Giotto*, named for the fourteenth-century painter who had depicted Halley's comet as the star of Bethlehem. *Giotto* had been programmed to fly through the comet's tail and behind the nucleus. In this way, it would be able to take photos of the highest possible clarity.

The photos were taken from a distance of 370 miles (592 kilometers) from the nucleus and showed it to be a velvet black lump about 9.4 by 6.2 miles (15 by 10 kilometers) in size. The nucleus was spewing jets of water vapor and dust. As *Giotto* flew through the comet's tail, each second it was showered by one hundred dust particles the size of grains of sand.

The Giotto *space probe, launched in 1985, brushed past the hidden nucleus of Halley's comet in 1986. Its camera recorded many images that gave scientists a unique opportunity to increase their knowledge of Halley.*

After sending more than 2,000 photos back to earth, *Giotto* went silent. Thirty-four minutes later, it resumed contact with earth. Everything but the camera was working. No matter—*Giotto* had already fulfilled its mission.

DEATH OF A STAR

Astronomers remember 1987 as "the year of the supernova." It was the first time in almost 400 years that a supernova, the death of a star, had been seen unaided from earth. The only prior instance in which a supernova was visible to the naked eye was in 1604, when astronomer Johannes Kepler witnessed the event.

Early on the morning of February 24, two astronomers in Chile, Ian Shelton of the University of Toronto Southern Station and Oscar Duhalde of

An image of the area around the Tarantula nebula (top left) *in the Large Magellanic Cloud, showing the supernova 1987a, the brighter star at bottom right*

Las Campanas Observatory, observed and reported the phenomenon. So did Albert Jones, an amateur astronomer in Nelson, New Zealand. All three observations were made in the Southern Hemisphere, the only area from which the event could be seen. The supernova itself was located in the Large Magellanic Cloud, a satellite of earth's galaxy, the Milky Way.

As a star forms, it changes hydrogen into helium and then to heavier and heavier elements. In time, the core of the star is converted into iron. However, by that time, the core is unable to release energy to support the star's structure. This causes the center of the star to collapse inward on itself.

This in turn produces a violent outward shock wave and gigantic explosion. A stunning event, the explosion creates light that is one hundred billion times brighter than the sun. Within a few months, this spectacular light show gradually begins to fade from view.

Space Exploration to Advance Human Welfare

Two major events in 1988 were intended to refocus efforts in outer space exploration as a means of advancing human welfare and world peace. The National Research Council recommended some major changes in its preview of space science in the twenty-first century. Among the changes was a shift in priorities from large engineering projects "for their own sake" to projects that would advance science and its applications to human welfare.

On May 31, President Ronald Reagan of the United States and the head of the Soviet Union, Mikhail Gorbachev, signed an agreement to extend earlier efforts by the two nations in the exploration and use of outer space for peaceful purposes. The two leaders agreed to exchange flight opportunities, place instruments on each nation's spacecraft, and share data on missions to the planets.

In 1992, American and Russian officials signed a flight opportunity agreement whereby Russian astronauts would join their American counterparts in space shuttle missions and American astronauts would spend time on the Russian space station *Mir*.

The launching of a United States space shuttle in February 1994 with a Russian astronaut aboard marked the first time this had ever happened. In 1995, plans called for placing an American astronaut aboard the *Mir* space station for a mission that would last ninety days.

This happened on March 14, 1995, when an American astronaut, fifty-one-year-old Dr. Norman E. Thagard, became the first American to ride into space in a Russian rocket and join Russian astronauts in the *Mir* space station for a three-month study on how humans adapt to weightlessness. Dr. Thagard was a United States Marine fighter pilot during the Vietnam War before becoming a medical doctor and then an astronaut.

The Risks of Space Travel

The majority of missions to outer space had passed without any harmful incidents, but every once in a while something would go wrong, as if to remind observers that whenever anyone travels to outer space, risks are involved. This was the case on September 6, 1988, when the crew of the Soviet spacecraft *Soyuz TM-6* was almost marooned in orbit because of equipment failure and crew errors.

Vladimir Lyakhov and Valery Polyakov of the Soviet Union and Abdul Ahad Mohmand of Afghanistan had spent nine days aboard the Soviet space station *Mir* when Lyakhov and Mohmand prepared to return to earth. Polyakov, who was a physician, would remain aboard *Mir* to monitor the health of two other Soviet cosmonauts, Titov and Manarov, who had been aboard the space station since December 1987.

Once aboard their *Soyuz* spacecraft, the three men attempted to fire the retro-rockets. They were thwarted, however, when a piece of altitude-control equipment malfunctioned. Three hours later, they attempted a second firing, but it lasted only 6 seconds instead of the necessary 230. This happened because the onboard computer had not been reset properly.

Compounding the error, Lyakhov refired the engine manually. This complicated the reentry calculations because of the changes in orbit. The decision was then made to postpone the third refiring so ground controllers could analyze the problem.

Meanwhile Lyakhov and Mohmand waited anxiously. They had only forty-eight hours of air and water when they left *Mir*. Fortunately one other option still remained to them. They could make a manually controlled reentry almost anywhere if that became necessary. However, this did not become necessary and they returned safely to earth on September 7, 1988.

SURPRISES FROM THE NEPTUNE FLYBY

When the United States spacecraft *Voyager 2* was launched in 1977, it was intended to fly by Jupiter and Saturn and transmit photos and other data to scientists on earth. But twelve years later, in a rare occurrence, the planets, in their orbits, had reached such positions in space that *Voyager* could also be aimed to fly by Uranus in 1986 and Neptune in 1989.

The first close look at Neptune brought a number of surprises. A pale blue planet, its most notable feature was a Great Dark Spot the size of earth. There were only a few white clouds circling the planet, but they were moving at 400 miles (640 kilometers) per hour, in a direction that was opposite to the planet's rotation!

The biggest surprise *Voyager* revealed was that Neptune's moon Triton,

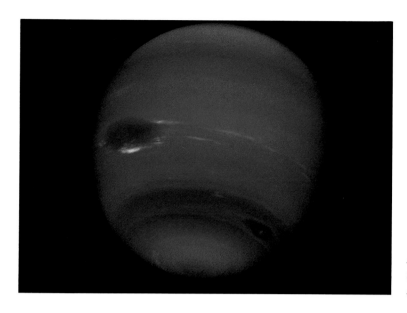

Neptune, the blue planet, is the farthest planet from the sun during part of its orbit.

one of eight that orbit the planet, turned out to be smaller and brighter than scientists had expected. Data revealed a thin nitrogen atmosphere and volcanoes of liquid nitrogen on Triton. Surface temperature was -400°F (-240°C), making Triton one of the coldest objects in the solar system.

Advances in television transmission in 1989 included a weeklong series of relayed photos from the *Voyager 2* space probe as it approached and flew by Neptune. TV viewers could see the pictures and hear of *Voyager*'s discoveries almost as soon as the scientists at NASA had made their analyses.

Further Reading

Asimov, Isaac. *How Did We Find Out About Neptune?* New York: Walker, 1990.

Byczynski, Lynn. *Genetics: Nature's Blueprints.* San Diego: Lucent, 1991.

Cheney, Glenn A. *Chernobyl: The Ongoing Story of the World's Deadliest Nuclear Disaster.* New York: Macmillan, 1994.

Cousins, Margaret. *The Story of Thomas Alva Edison.* New York: Random House, 1981.

Ford, Michael. *One Hundred Questions and Answers about AIDS: What You Need to Know Now.* New York: Morrow, 1993.

Hare, Tony. *Rainforest Destruction.* New York: Simon and Schuster, 1990.

Hill, John. *Exploring Information Technology.* Chatham, N.J.: Raintree Steck-Vaughn, 1992.

Johnson, Rebecca L. *Diving into Darkness: A Submersible Explores the Sea.* Minneapolis: Lerner, 1989.

Kronenwetter, Michael. *Managing Toxic Wastes.* New York: Simon and Schuster, 1989.

Lampton, Christopher. *Hurricane.* Brookfield, Conn.: Millbrook, 1991.

Lauber, Patricia. *Volcano: The Eruption and Healing of Mount St. Helens.* New York: Macmillan, 1986.

Mactire, Sean P. *Lyme Disease and Other Pest-Borne Illnesses.* New York: Franklin Watts, 1991.

Markle, Sandra. *Pioneering Ocean Depths.* New York: Macmillan, 1995.

Parker, Steve. *Charles Darwin and Evolution.* New York: HarperCollins, 1992.

Silverstein, Alvin, and Virginia B. Silverstein. *AIDS: Deadly Threat.* Hillside, N.J.: Enslow, 1991.

Skurzynski, Gloria. *Robots: Your High-Tech World.* New York: Macmillan, 1990.

Tangley, Laura. *The Rainforest.* New York: Chelsea House, 1992.

Tyson, Peter. *Acid Rain.* New York: Chelsea House, 1992.

Verba, Joan M. *Voyager: Exploring the Outer Planets.* Minneapolis: Lerner, 1991.

Waters, John F. *Deep-Sea Vents: Living Worlds Without Sun.* New York: Dutton, 1994.

White, Ryan, and Ann M. Cunningham. *Ryan White: My Own Story.* New York: Dial Books for Young Readers, 1991.

Wilcox, Frank H. *DNA: The Thread of Life.* Minneapolis: Lerner, 1988.

Winter, Frank H. *Comet Watch: The Return of Halley's Comet.* Minneapolis: Lerner, 1986.

Index

References to illustrations are listed in *italic, **boldface*** type.

acid rain, 22
AIDS, 29, 32–35
aircraft, supersonic, 55–56
Alvin (research submarine), 24
Amazon rain forests, 15–16, 17
Argo (underwater search vehicle), 52, 53
artificial intelligence, 45
aspirin, 29, 36–37, 40–41
automobiles
    computers in, 43–44, *44*
    electric, 51

Berg, Paul, 29–30
birdsongs, 17–18
blood transfusions, 33, 34, 35
Bossert, Patrick, 51
Boyer, Herbert, 30, *31*
buildings, energy-saving, 49–50

caiman, 16, *16*
cancer, 15, 21, 28, 32, 34, 40
carbon dioxide, 10, 13, 14, 23, 24

Carter, Jimmy, 49
CD-ROM, 43, 45–46
Chernobyl nuclear plant, 26–28
cholesterol, 37–38, *38*
chromosomes, 39, *39*
climatologists, 10
Cohen, Stanley, 30, *31*
Collins, Francis, 41
comets, 59
computers, 43–48
    viruses, 46–48
Concorde, 55–56
condoms, 33, 35
cystic fibrosis, 41

Darwin, Charles, 19
Dausset, Jean, 30
disasters
    geophysical, 23–24
    industrial, 22–23
    nuclear, 26–28
DNA fingerprinting, 39–40

Edison, Thomas, 50, *50*
electricity, 50–51
elephants, 18–19

El Niño, 12
Eurotunnel, 54–55, *55*
Evans, Clifford, 17
evolution, theory of, 19, 20
extraterrestrials, 62
Exxon Valdez, 25

Field Guide to the Birds, 18
Fullerton, C. Gordon, 59

gene splicing, 30
gene therapy, 41
Gilbert, Walter, 29–30
Giotto, 57, 66–67, *67*
Gorbachev, Mikhail, 69
Gould, Stephen Jay, 20, *20*
Graybill, Donald, 14
greenhouse effect, 9, 13–15, 58

Halley's comet, 57, 63, 65–66, *67*
Hauser, Susan, 11
heart attacks, 29, 32, 40–41
hemophilia, 29
HIV. *See* AIDS.
Hurricane Hugo, 12–13, *13*

insecticides, 17
interferon, 30, 58

Jewitt, David, 65
Jones, Albert, 68
Jones, Philip, 14

Karsh, Karl, 32
Kazakov, Vasily S., 28

Kelly, Mick, 14
Kepler, Johannes, 67
Knorr (research vessel), 52
Koop, C. Everett, 35

Lake Nyos, 23–24
Leakey, Richard, 19
Love Canal, 21
Lyakhov, Vladimir, 70
Lyme disease, 38, 52

Mars, 62–63, 65
Mars Observer, 63
McAuliffe, Christa, 64, *64*
memory chips, 45, *45*
mentally ill, treatment of, 36
mice, 40
Mohmand, Abdul Ahad, 70
Moss, Cynthia, 19
Mount Saint Helens, 9–10, *10*, 11

NASA, 56, 63, 64, 65, 71
natural selection, theory of, 19
Nelson, Todd E., 59
Neptune, 70–71, *71*

oil spills, 21, 25–26
Orient Express, 56
otter, *25*
ozone layer, 9, 15

Paine, Thomas, 65
Peterson, Roger Tory, 18, *18*
Pioneer 10, 62
Pioneer-Venus, 58, 59, 63, 66

Pitchfork, Colin, 40
plant geneticists, 17
pollution, 9, 22, 51
Polyakov, Valery, 70
Popov, Leonid, 57–58

Quinlan, Karen Ann, 37

Reagan, Ronald, 65, 69
Reye's syndrome, 36–37
Ride, Sally, 57, 61, *61*
riftia worms, 24, *24*
Riordan, John, 41
robots, 53, 54
rocket backpack, 61–62
Ross, Jerry, 63
Rubik, Erno, 51
Rubik's Cube, 51
Ryumin, Valeri, 57–58

Sagan, Carl, 62
Sanger, Frederick, 29–30
satellites
    communications, 57, 61, 63–64
    search-and-rescue, 51–52
sex education, 35
Sloan, John, 18
Snell, George, 30
Soyuz TM-6, 70
spacecraft. *See specific craft.*
space shuttles
    Atlantis, 63
    Challenger, 57, 61, 64
    Columbia, 59

space stations, 57, 63, 65
    Mir, 65, 69, 70
    Salyut 6, 57, 58
Spring, Sherwood, 63
strokes, 41
sulfur dioxide, 10, 14, 22
supernova, 67–68, *68*
Swan, Joseph, 50

Tarantula nebula, *68*
Telyatnikov, Leonid, *27*
test tube twins, 31
Thagard, Norman E., 69
Titanic, 52–53, *53*
Triton, 70–71
toxic gas, 22–23
toxic wastes, 9, 20–21
trees, 14, 15, 17

ultraviolet radiation, 9, 15
Union Carbide factory, *22*

Vega 1 and *2*, 66
Venera 13, 60
Venus, 58, *58*, 59, 60, 65
Viking, 63
volcanoes, 9–11, 23, 24
Voyager 2, 70–71

weather, 10–11, 12
Whipple, Fred, 66
White, Ryan, *34*, 35
Woodward, Frank, 14

About the Author

Robert E. Dunbar lives in Damariscotta in mid-coastal Maine. He is the author of fifteen published books. These include books on zoology, heredity, mental retardation, and the heart and circulatory system. In addition to his work as a writer, Mr. Dunbar occasionally substitutes as a teacher at nearby Lincoln Academy, a private school that serves as a regional high school. He serves as a judge at high school debate and speech competitions and in the state and district finals of the National Forensic League and Catholic Forensic League.

From time to time, Mr. Dunbar performs as singer and actor in concerts and musical and dramatic works produced locally and in nearby towns. He has written the books for three musical comedies: "Vaudeville Gold," "Friends and Lovers," and "Folk and Fancy."